Seven Discourses
On Art

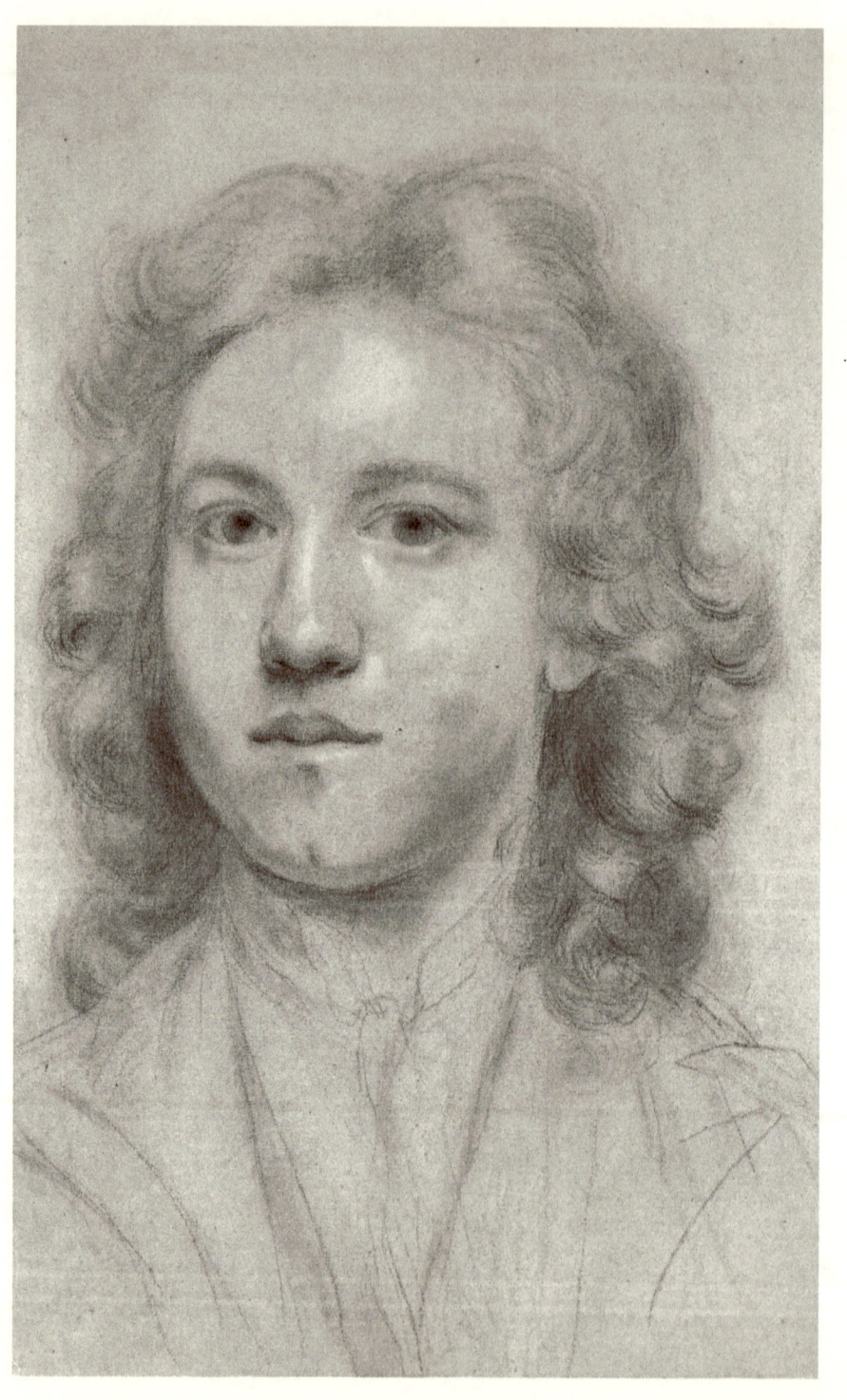

Seven Discourses On Art

Sir Joshua Reynolds

PERUSE PRESS
LOS ANGELES

Title: Seven Discourses on Art

Author: Sir Joshua Reynolds

Transcribed from the 1901
Cassell and Company edition

Editor: Mark Diederichsen

Publisher: Peruse Press
Los Angeles, California

First Peruse Press edition
First printing 2013

Front cover painting:
Joshua Reynolds and studio
Sarah Siddons as the Tragic Muse
1789
oil on canvas
2,397 x 1,476mm (94 x 58 in.)
commissioned by Noel Desenfans
Dulwich Picture Gallery, London
(after the 1784 original version by Reynolds
in the Huntington Library, San Marino)

Frontispiece:
Joshua Reynolds
Self Portrait (age 17)
circa 1740
charcoal and white chalk and stump, on buff laid paper
Private collection

Back cover painting:
Joshua Reynolds
Self-portrait
circa 1747-9
oil on canvas
635 x 743mm (25 x 29 in.)
National Portrait Gallery, London.

ISBN-13: 978-0615850832
ISBN-10: 0615850839

CONTENTS

◇◇◇◇◇◇◇◇◇◇◇◇◇◇◇

ILLUSTRATIONS

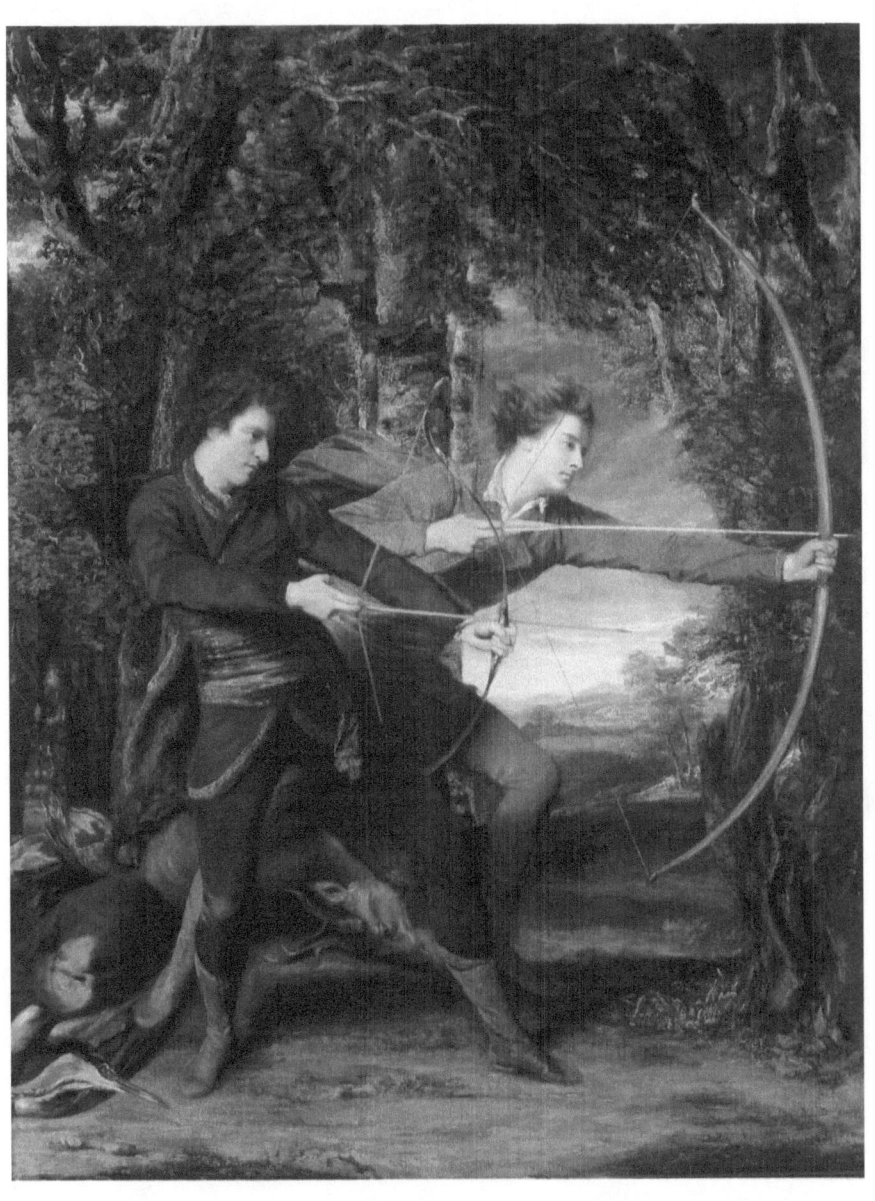

Joshua Reynolds
Colonel Acland and Lord Sydney: The Archers
1769
oil on canvas, 236 x 180 cm
Tate Britain

◇◇◇◇◇◇◇◇◇◇◇◇◇◇◇◇

INTRODUCTION

I t is a happy memory that associates the foundation of our Royal Academy with the delivery of these inaugural discourses by Sir Joshua Reynolds, on the opening of the schools, and at the first annual meetings for the distribution of its prizes. They laid down principles of art from the point of view of a man of genius who had made his power felt, and with the clear good sense which is the foundation of all work that looks upward and may hope to live. The truths here expressed concerning Art may, with slight adjustment of the way of thought, be applied to Literature or to any exercise of the best powers of mind for shaping the delights that raise us to the larger sense of life. In his separation of the utterance of whole truths from insistence upon accidents of detail, Reynolds was right, because he guarded the expression of his view with careful definitions of its limits. In the same way Boileau was right, as a critic of Literature, in demanding everywhere good sense, in condemning the paste brilliants of a style then in decay, and fixing attention upon the masterly simplicity of Roman poets in the time of Augustus. Critics by rule of thumb reduced the principles clearly defined by Boileau to a dull convention, against which there came in course of time a strong reaction. In like manner the teaching of Reynolds was applied by dull men to much vague and conventional generalisation in the name of dignity. Nevertheless, Reynolds taught essential truths of Art. The principles laid down by him will never fail to give strength to the right artist, or true guidance towards the appreciation of good art, though here and there we may not wholly assent to some passing application of them, where the difference may be great between a fashion of thought in his time and in ours. A righteous enforcement of exact truth in our day has led many into a readiness to appreciate more really the minute imitation of a satin dress, or a red herring, than the noblest figure in the best of Raffaelle's cartoons. Much good should come of the diffusion of this wise little book.

Joshua Reynolds was born on the 15th of July, 1723, the son of a clergyman and schoolmaster, at Plympton in Devonshire. His bent for Art was clear and strong from his childhood. In 1741 at the age of nineteen, he began study, and studied for two yours in London under Thomas Hudson, a successful portrait painter. Then he went back to

Devonshire and painted portraits, aided for some time in his education by attention to the work of William Gandy of Exeter. When twenty-six years old, in May, 1749, Reynolds was taken away by Captain Keppel to the Mediterranean, and brought into contact with the works of the great painters of Italy. He stayed two years in Rome, and in accordance with the principles afterwards laid down in these lectures, he refused, when in Rome, commissions for copying, and gave his mind to minute observation of the art of the great masters by whose works he was surrounded. He spent two months in Florence, six weeks in Venice, a few days in Bologna and Parma. "If," he said, "I had never seen any of the fine works of Correggio, I should never, perhaps, have remarked in Nature the expression which I find in one of his pieces; or if I had remarked it, I might have thought it too difficult, or perhaps impossible to execute."

In 1753 Reynolds came back to England, and stayed three months in Devonshire before setting up a studio in London, in St. Martin's Lane, which was then an artists' quarter. His success was rapid. In 1755 he had one hundred and twenty-five sitters. Samuel Johnson found in him his most congenial friend. He moved to Newport Street, and he built himself a studio—where there is now an auction room—at 47, Lincoln's Inn Fields. There he remained for life.

In 1760 the artists opened, in a room lent by the Society of Arts, a free Exhibition for the sale of their works. This was continued the next year at Spring Gardens, with a charge of a shilling for admission. In 1765 they obtained a charter of incorporation, and in 1768 the King gave his support to the foundation of a Royal Academy of Arts by seceders from the preceding "Incorporated Society of Artists," into which personal feelings had brought much division. It was to consist, like the French Academy, of forty members, and was to maintain Schools open to all students of good character who could give evidence that they had fully learnt the rudiments of Art. The foundation by the King dates from the 10th of December, 1768. The Schools were opened on the 2nd of January next following, and on that occasion Joshua Reynolds, who had been elected President—his age was then between forty-five and forty-six—gave the Inaugural Address which formed the first of these Seven Discourses. The other six were given by him, as President, at the next six annual meetings: and they were all shaped to form, when collected into a volume, a coherent body of good counsel upon the foundations of the painter's art.

INTRODUCTION

TO THE KING

The regular progress of cultivated life is from necessaries to accommodations, from accommodations to ornaments. By your illustrious predecessors were established marts for manufactures, and colleges for science; but for the arts of elegance, those arts by which manufactures are embellished and science is refined, to found an academy was reserved for your Majesty.

Had such patronage been without effect, there had been reason to believe that nature had, by some insurmountable impediment, obstructed our proficiency; but the annual improvement of the exhibitions which your Majesty has been pleased to encourage shows that only encouragement had been wanting.

To give advice to those who are contending for royal liberality has been for some years the duty of my station in the Academy; and these Discourses hope for your Majesty's acceptance as well-intended endeavours to incite that emulation which your notice has kindled, and direct those studies which your bounty has rewarded.

May it please your Majesty,
Your Majesty's
Most dutiful servant,
And most faithful subject,

JOSHUA REYNOLDS.

TO THE MEMBERS OF THE ROYAL ACADEMY.

Gentlemen, — That you have ordered the publication of this Discourse is not only very flattering to me, as it implies your approbation of the method of study which I have recommended; but likewise, as this method receives from that act such an additional weight and authority as demands from the students that deference and respect, which can be due only to the united sense of so considerable a body of artists.

I am,
With the greatest esteem and respect,
GENTLEMEN,
Your most humble
And obedient servant,

JOSHUA REYNOLDS.

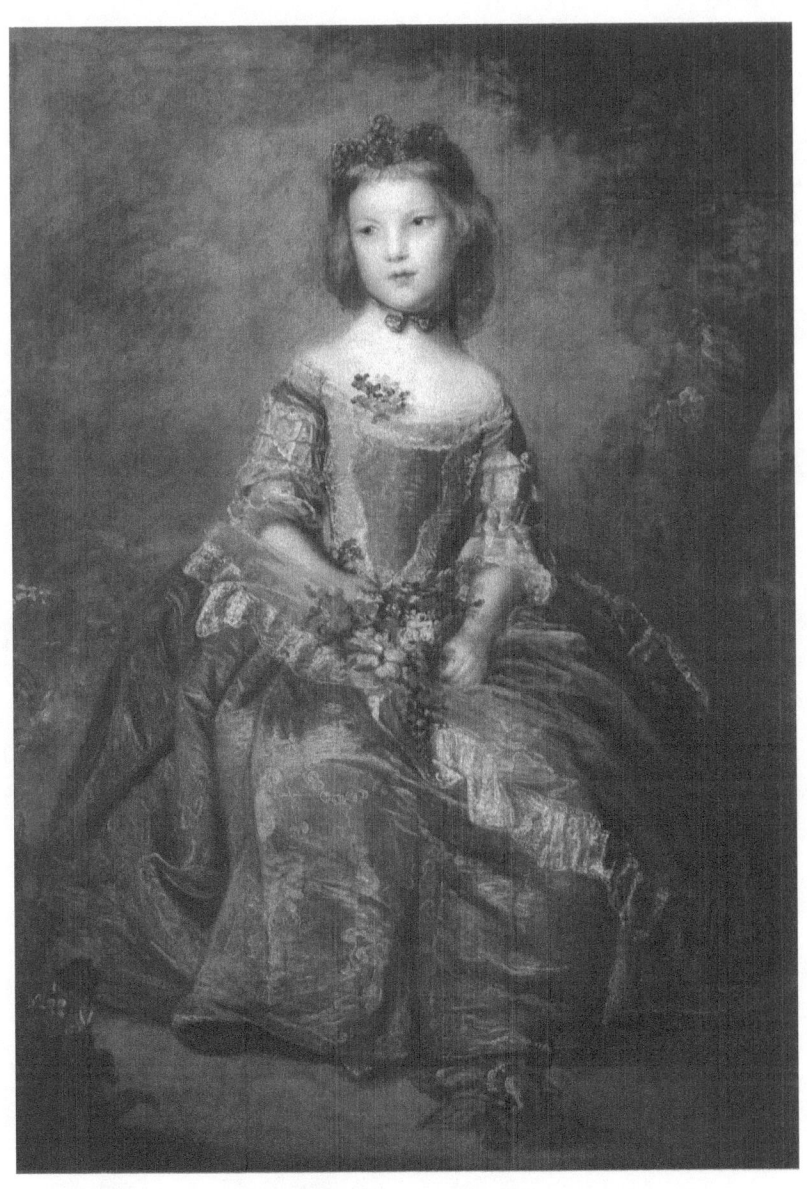

Joshua Reynolds
Lady Elizabeth Hamilton
1758
oil on canvas, 117 x 84 cm
Widener Collection
National Gallery of Art, Washington

DISCOURSE I

Delivered at the Opening of the Royal Academy
January 2nd, 1769
by the President

G entlemen, — An academy in which the polite arts may be regularly cultivated is at last opened among us by royal munificence. This must appear an event in the highest degree interesting, not only to the artists, but to the whole nation.

It is indeed difficult to give any other reason why an Empire like that of Britain should so long have wanted an ornament so suitable to its greatness than that slow progression of things which naturally makes elegance and refinement the last effect of opulence and power.

An institution like this has often been recommended upon considerations merely mercantile. But an academy founded upon such principles can never effect even its own narrow purposes. If it has an origin no higher, no taste can ever be formed in it which can be useful even in manufactures; but if the higher arts of design flourish, these inferior ends will be answered of course.

We are happy in having a prince who has conceived the design of such an institution, according to its true dignity, and promotes the arts, as the head of a great, a learned, a polite, and a commercial nation; and I can now congratulate you, gentlemen, on the accomplishment of your long and ardent wishes.

The numberless and ineffectual consultations that I have had with many in this assembly, to form plans and concert schemes for an academy, afford a sufficient proof of the impossibility of succeeding but by the influence of Majesty. But there have, perhaps, been times when even the influence of Majesty would have been ineffectual, and it is pleasing to reflect that we are thus embodied, when every circumstance seems to concur from which honour and prosperity can probably arise.

There are at this time a greater number of excellent artists than were ever known before at one period in this nation; there is a general desire among our nobility to be distinguished as lovers and judges of the arts; there is a greater superfluity of wealth among the people to reward the professors; and, above all, we are patronised by a monarch, who, knowing the value of science and of elegance, thinks every art worthy of his notice that tends to soften and humanise the mind.

After so much has been done by his Majesty, it will be wholly our fault if our progress is not in some degree correspondent to the wisdom and, generosity of the institution; let us show our gratitude in our diligence, that, though our merit may not answer his expectations, yet, at least, our industry may deserve his protection.

But whatever may be our proportion of success, of this we may be sure, that the present institution will at least contribute to advance our knowledge of the arts, and bring us nearer to that ideal excellence which it is the lot of genius always to contemplate and never to attain.

The principal advantage of an academy is, that, besides furnishing able men to direct the student, it will be a repository for the great examples of the art. These are the materials on which genius is to work, and without which the strongest intellect may be fruitlessly or deviously employed. By studying these authentic models, that idea of excellence which is the result of the accumulated experience of past ages may be at once acquired, and the tardy and obstructed progress of our predecessors may teach us a shorter and easier way. The student receives at one glance the principles which many artists have spent their whole lives in ascertaining; and, satisfied with their effect, is spared the painful investigation by which they come to be known and fixed. How many men of great natural abilities have been lost to this nation for want of these advantages? They never had an opportunity of seeing those masterly efforts of genius which at once kindle the whole soul, and force it into sudden and irresistible approbation.

Raffaelle, it is true, had not the advantage of studying in an academy; but all Rome, and the works of Michael Angelo in particular, were to him an academy. On the site of the Capel la Sistina he immediately from a dry, Gothic, and even insipid manner, which attends to the minute accidental discriminations of particular and individual objects, assumed that grand style of painting, which improves partial representation by the general and invariable ideas of nature.

Every seminary of learning may be said to be surrounded with an atmosphere of floating knowledge, where every mind may imbibe somewhat congenial to its own original conceptions. Knowledge, thus obtained, has always something more popular and useful than that

which is forced upon the mind by private precepts or solitary meditation. Besides, it is generally found that a youth more easily receives
instruction from the companions of his studies, whose minds are nearly
on a level with his own, than from those who are much his superiors;
and it is from his equals only that he catches the fire of emulation.

One advantage, I will venture to affirm, we shall have in our
academy, which no other nation can boast. We shall have nothing to
unlearn. To this praise the present race of artists have a just claim. As
far as they have yet proceeded they are right. With us the exertions of
genius will henceforward be directed to their proper objects. It will
not be as it has been in other schools, where he that travelled fastest
only wandered farthest from the right way.

Impressed as I am, therefore, with such a favourable opinion of
my associates in this undertaking, it would ill become me to dictate
to any of them. But as these institutions have so often failed in other
nations, and as it is natural to think with regret how much might have
been done, and how little has been done, I must take leave to offer a
few hints, by which those errors may be rectified, and those defects
supplied. These the professors and visitors may reject or adopt as they
shall think proper.

I would chiefly recommend that an implicit obedience to the rules
of art, as established by the great masters, should be exacted from
the *young* students. That those models, which have passed through
the approbation of ages, should be considered by them as perfect and
infallible guides as subjects for their imitation, not their criticism.

I am confident that this is the only efficacious method of making
a progress in the arts; and that he who sets out with doubting will
find life finished before he becomes master of the rudiments. For it
may be laid down as a maxim, that he who begins by presuming on
his own sense has ended his studies as soon as he has commenced
them. Every opportunity, therefore, should be taken to discounte-
nance that false and vulgar opinion that rules are the fetters of genius.
They are fetters only to men of no genius; as that armour, which upon
the strong becomes an ornament and a defence, upon the weak and
misshapen turns into a load, and cripples the body which it was made
to protect.

How much liberty may be taken to break through those rules,
and, as the poet expresses it,

"To snatch a grace beyond the reach of art," may be an after consideration, when the pupils become masters themselves. It is then, when their genius has received its utmost improvement, that rules may possibly be dispensed with. But let us not destroy the scaffold until we have raised the building.

The directors ought more particularly to watch over the genius of those students who, being more advanced, are arrived at that critical period of study, on the nice management of which their future turn of taste depends. At that age it is natural for them to be more captivated with what is brilliant than with what is solid, and to prefer splendid negligence to painful and humiliating exactness.

A facility in composing, a lively, and what is called a masterly handling the chalk or pencil, are, it must be confessed, captivating qualities to young minds, and become of course the objects of their ambition. They endeavour to imitate those dazzling excellences, which they will find no great labour in attaining. After much time spent in these frivolous pursuits, the difficulty will be to retreat; but it will be then too late; and there is scarce an instance of return to scrupulous labour after the mind has been debauched and deceived by this fallacious mastery.

By this useless industry they are excluded from all power of advancing in real excellence. Whilst boys, they are arrived at their utmost perfection; they have taken the shadow for the substance; and make that mechanical facility the chief excellence of the art, which is only an ornament, and of the merit of which few but painters themselves are judges.

This seems to me to be one of the most dangerous sources of corruption; and I speak of it from experience, not as an error which may possibly happen, but which has actually infected all foreign academies. The directors were probably pleased with this premature dexterity in their pupils, and praised their despatch at the expense of their correctness.

But young men have not only this frivolous ambition of being thought masterly inciting them on one hand, but also their natural sloth tempting them on the other. They are terrified at the prospect before them, of the toil required to attain exactness. The impetuosity of youth is distrusted at the slow approaches of a regular siege, and desires, from mere impatience of labour, to take the citadel by storm. They wish to find some shorter path to excellence, and hope to obtain the reward of eminence by other means than those which the indispensable rules of art have prescribed. They must, therefore, be told again and again that labour is the only price of solid fame, and that whatever their force of genius may be, there is no easy method of becoming a good painter.

When we read the lives of the most eminent painters, every page informs us that no part of their time was spent in dissipation. Even an increase of fame served only to augment their industry. To be convinced with what persevering assiduity they pursued their studies, we need only reflect on their method of proceeding in their most celebrated works. When they conceived a subject, they first made a variety of sketches; then a finished drawing of the whole; after that a more correct drawing of every separate part, heads, hands, feet, and pieces of drapery; they then painted the picture, and after all retouched it from the life. The pictures, thus wrought with such pain, now appear like the effect of enchantment, and as if some mighty genius had struck them off at a blow.

But, whilst diligence is thus recommended to the students, the visitors will take care that their diligence be effectual; that it be well directed and employed on the proper object. A student is not always advancing because he is employed; he must apply his strength to that part of the art where the real difficulties lie; to that part which distinguishes it as a liberal art, and not by mistaken industry lose his time in that which is merely ornamental. The students, instead of vying with each other which shall have the readiest band, should be taught to contend who shall have the purest and most correct outline, instead of striving which shall produce the brightest tint, or, curiously trifling endeavour to give the gloss of stuffs so as to appear real, let their ambition be directed to contend which shall dispose his drapery in the most graceful folds, which shall give the most grace and dignity to the human figure.

I must beg leave to submit one thing more to the consideration of the visitors, which appears to me a matter of very great consequence, and the omission of which I think a principal defect in the method of education pursued in all the academies I have ever visited. The error I mean is, that the students never draw exactly from the living models which they have before them. It is not indeed their intention, nor are they directed to do it. Their drawings resemble the model only in the attitude. They change the form according to their vague and uncertain ideas of beauty, and make a drawing rather of what they think the figure ought to be than of what it appears. I have thought this the obstacle that has stopped the progress of many young men of real genius; and I very much doubt whether a habit of drawing correctly what we see will not give a proportionable power of drawing correctly what we imagine. He who endeavours to copy nicely the figure before him not only acquires a habit of exactness and precision, but is continually advancing in his knowledge of the human figure; and though he seems to superficial observers to make a slower progress, he will be found at last capable of adding (without running into capricious wildness) that grace and beauty which is necessary to be given to his more finished works, and which cannot be got by the moderns, as it was not acquired by the ancients, but by an attentive and well-compared study of the human form.

What I think ought to enforce this method is, that it has been the practice (as may be seen by their drawings) of the great masters in the art. I will mention a drawing of Raffaelle, "The Dispute of the Sacrament," the print of which, by Count Cailus, is in every hand. It appears that he made his sketch from one model; and the habit he had of drawing exactly from the form before him appears by his making all the figures with the same cap, such as his model then happened to wear; so servile a copyist was this great man, even at a time when he was allowed to be at his highest pitch of excellence.

I have seen also academy figures by Annibale Caracci, though he was often sufficiently licentious in his finished works, drawn with all the peculiarities of an individual model.

This scrupulous exactness is so contrary to the practice of the academies, that it is not without great deference that I beg leave to recommend it to the consideration of the visitors, and submit it to them, whether the neglect of this method is not one of the reasons why students so often disappoint expectation, and being more than boys at sixteen, become less than men at thirty.

In short, the method I recommend can only be detrimental when there are but few living forms to copy; for then students, by always drawing from one alone, will by habit be taught to overlook defects, and mistake deformity for beauty. But of this there is no danger, since the council has determined to supply the academy with a variety of subjects; and indeed those laws which they have drawn up, and which the secretary will presently read for your confirmation, have in some measure precluded me from saying more upon this occasion. Instead, therefore, of offering my advice, permit me to indulge my wishes, and express my hope, that this institution may answer the expectations of its royal founder; that the present age may vie in arts with that of Leo X, and that "the dignity of the dying art" (to make use of an expression of Pliny) may be revived under the reign of George III.

Joshua Reynolds
Captain John Foote
1761–1765
oil on canvas, 123.2 x 99 cm
York Museums Trust

Joshua Reynolds
Admiral Augustus Keppel
1779
oil on canvas, 127 x 101.6 cm
National Maritime Museum

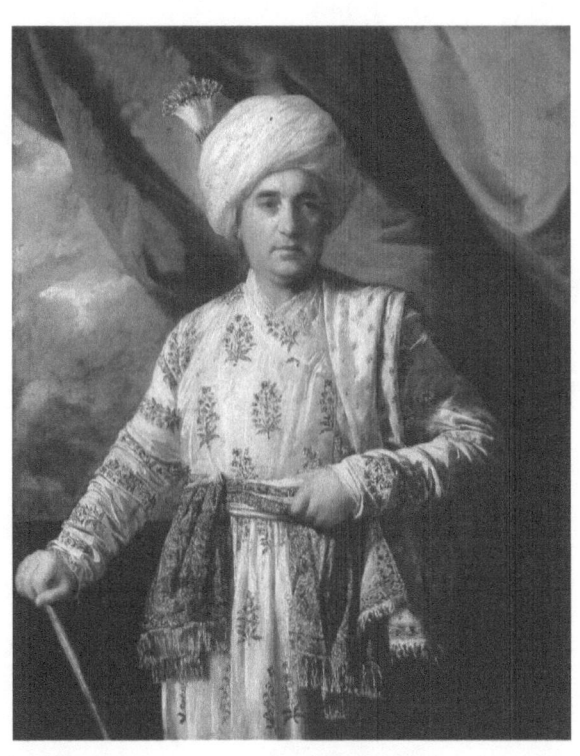

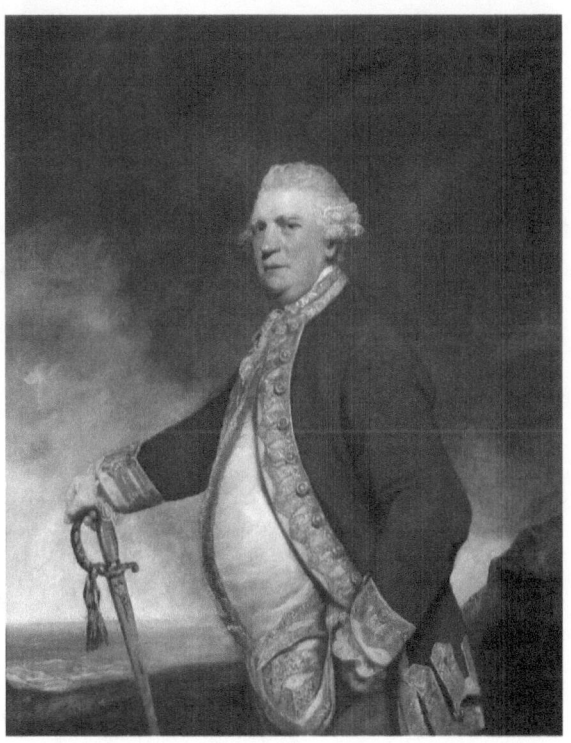

◇◇◇◇◇◇◇◇◇◇◇◇◇◇
DISCOURSE II

**Delivered to the Students of the Royal Academy
on the Distribution of the Prizes
December 11, 1769
by the President**

Gentlemen, — I congratulate you on the honour which you have just received. I have the highest opinion of your merits, and could wish to show my sense of them in something which possibly may be more useful to you than barren praise. I could wish to lead you into such a course of study as may render your future progress answerable to your past improvement; and, whilst I applaud you for what has been done, remind you of how much yet remains to attain perfection.

I flatter myself, that from the long experience I have had, and the unceasing assiduity with which I have pursued those studies, in which, like you, I have been engaged, I shall be acquitted of vanity in offering some hints to your consideration. They are indeed in a great degree founded upon my own mistakes in the same pursuit. But the history of errors properly managed often shortens the road to truth. And although no method of study that I can offer will of itself conduct to excellence, yet it may preserve industry from being misapplied.

In speaking to you of the theory of the art, I shall only consider it as it has a relation to the method of your studies.

Dividing the study of painting into three distinct periods, I shall address you as having passed through the first of them, which is confined to the rudiments, including a facility of drawing any object that presents itself, a tolerable readiness in the management of colours, and an acquaintance with the most simple and obvious rules of composition.

This first degree of proficiency is, in painting, what grammar is in literature, a general preparation to whatever species of the art the student may afterwards choose for his more particular application. The power of drawing, modelling, and using colours is very properly called the language of the art; and in this language, the honours you have just received prove you to have made no inconsiderable progress.

When the artist is once enabled to express himself with some degree of correctness, he must then endeavour to collect subjects for expression; to amass a stock of ideas, to be combined and varied as occasion may require. He is now in the second period of study, in which his business is to learn all that has hitherto been known and done. Having hitherto received instructions from a particular master, he is now to consider the art itself as his master. He must extend his capacity to more sublime and general instructions. Those perfections which lie scattered among various masters are now united in one general idea, which is henceforth to regulate his taste and enlarge his imagination. With a variety of models thus before him, he will avoid that narrowness and poverty of conception which attends a bigoted admiration of a single master, and will cease to follow any favourite where he ceases to excel. This period is, however, still a time of subjection and discipline. Though the student will not resign himself blindly to any single authority when he may have the advantage of consulting many, he must still be afraid of trusting his own judgment, and of deviating into any track where he cannot find the footsteps of some former master.

The third and last period emancipates the student from subjection to any authority but what he shall himself judge to be supported by reason. Confiding now in his own judgment, he will consider and separate those different principles to which different modes of beauty owe their original. In the former period he sought only to know and combine excellence, wherever it was to be found, into one idea of perfection; in this he learns, what requires the most attentive survey and the subtle disquisition, to discriminate perfections that are incompatible with each other.

He is from this time to regard himself as holding the same rank with those masters whom he before obeyed as teachers, and as exercising a sort of sovereignty over those rules which have hitherto restrained him. Comparing now no longer the performances of art with each other, but examining the art itself by the standard of nature, he corrects what is erroneous, supplies what is scanty, and adds by his own observation what the industry of his predecessors may have yet left wanting to perfection. Having well established his judgment, and stored his memory, he may now without fear try the power of his imagination. The mind that has been thus disciplined may be indulged in the warmest enthusiasm, and venture to play on the borders of the wildest extravagance. The habitual dignity, which long converse with the greatest minds has imparted to him, will display itself in all his attempts, and he will stand among his instructors, not as an imitator, but a rival.

These are the different stages of the art. But as I now address myself particularly to those students who have been this day rewarded for their happy passage through the first period, I can with no propriety suppose they want any help in the initiatory studies. My present design is to direct your view to distant excellence, and to show you the readiest path that leads to it. Of this I shall speak with such latitude as may leave the province of the professor uninvaded, and shall not anticipate those precepts which it is his business to give and your duty to understand.

It is indisputably evident that a great part of every man's life must be employed in collecting materials for the exercise of genius. Invention, strictly speaking, is little more than a new combination of those images which have been previously gathered and deposited in the memory. Nothing can come of nothing. He who has laid up no materials can produce no combinations.

A student unacquainted with the attempts of former adventurers is always apt to overrate his own abilities, to mistake the most trifling excursions for discoveries of moment, and every coast new to him for a new-found country. If by chance he passes beyond his usual limits, he congratulates his own arrival at those regions which they who have steered a better course have long left behind them.

The productions of such minds are seldom distinguished by an air of originality: they are anticipated in their happiest efforts; and if they are found to differ in anything from their predecessors, it is only in irregular sallies and trifling conceits. The more extensive therefore your acquaintance is with the works of those who have excelled the more extensive will be your powers of invention; and what may appear still more like a paradox, the more original will be your conceptions. But the difficulty on this occasion is to determine who ought to be proposed as models of excellence, and who ought to be considered as the properest guides.

To a young man just arrived in Italy, many of the present painters of that country are ready enough to obtrude their precepts, and to offer their own performances as examples of that perfection which they affect to recommend. The modern, however, who recommends *himself* as a standard, may justly be suspected as ignorant of the true end, and unacquainted with the proper object of the art which he professes. To follow such a guide will not only retard the student, but mislead him.

On whom, then, can he rely, or who shall show him the path that leads to excellence? The answer is obvious: Those great masters who have travelled the same road with success are the most likely to conduct others. The works of those who have stood the test of ages have a claim to that respect and veneration to which no modern can pretend. The duration and stability of their fame is sufficient to evince that it has not been suspended upon the slender thread of fashion and caprice, but bound to the human heart by every tie of sympathetic approbation.

There is no danger of studying too much the works of those great men, but how they may be studied to advantage is an inquiry of great importance.

Some who have never raised their minds to the consideration of the real dignity of the art, and who rate the works of an artist in proportion as they excel, or are defective in the mechanical parts, look on theory as something that may enable them to talk but not to paint better, and confining themselves entirely to mechanical practice, very assiduously toil on in the drudgery of copying, and think they make a rapid progress while they faithfully exhibit the minutest part of a favourite picture. This appears to me a very tedious, and I think a very erroneous, method of proceeding. Of every large composition, even of those which are most admired, a great part may be truly said to be commonplace. This, though it takes up much time in copying, conduces little to improvement. I consider general copying as a delusive kind of industry; the student satisfies himself with the appearance of doing something; he falls into the dangerous habit of imitating without selecting, and of labouring without any determinate object; as it requires no effort of the mind, he sleeps over his work; and those powers of invention and composition which ought particularly to be called out and put in action lie torpid, and lose their energy for want of exercise.

It is an observation that all must have made, how incapable those are of producing anything of their own who have spent much of their time in making finished copies.

To suppose that the complication of powers, and variety of ideas necessary to that mind which aspires to the first honours ill the art of painting, can be obtained by the frigid contemplation of a few single models, is no less absurd than it would be in him who wishes to be a poet to imagine that by translating a tragedy he can acquire to himself sufficient knowledge of the appearances of nature, the operations of the passions, and the incidents of life.

The great use in copying, if it be at all useful, should seem to be in learning to colour; yet even colouring will never be perfectly attained by servilely copying the mould before you. An eye critically nice can only be formed by observing well-coloured pictures with attention: and by close inspection, and minute examination you will discover, at last, the manner of handling, the artifices of contrast, glazing, and other expedients, by which good colourists have raised the value of their tints, and by which nature has been so happily imitated.

I must inform you, however, that old pictures deservedly celebrated for their colouring are often so changed by dirt and varnish, that we ought not to wonder if they do not appear equal to their reputation in the eyes of unexperienced painters, or young students. An artist whose judgment is matured by long observation, considers rather what the picture once was, than what it is at present. He has acquired a power by habit of seeing the brilliancy of tints through the cloud by which it is obscured. An exact imitation, therefore, of those pictures, is likely to fill the student's mind with false opinions, and to send him back a colourist of his own formation, with ideas equally remote from nature and from art, from the genuine practice of the masters and the real appearances of things.

Following these rules, and using these precautions, when you have clearly and distinctly learned in what good colouring consists, you cannot do better than have recourse to nature herself, who is always at hand, and in comparison of whose true splendour the best coloured pictures are but faint and feeble.

However, as the practice of copying is not entirely to be excluded, since the mechanical practice of painting is learned in some measure by it, let those choice parts only be selected which have recommended the work to notice. If its excellence consists in its general effect, it would be proper to make slight sketches of the machinery and general management of the picture. Those sketches should be kept always by you for the regulation of your style. Instead of copying the touches of those great masters, copy only their conceptions. Instead of treading in their footsteps, endeavour only to keep the same road. Labour to invent on their general principles and way of thinking. Possess yourself with their spirit. Consider with yourself how a Michael Angelo or a Raffaelle would have treated this subject: and work yourself into a belief that your picture is to be seen and criticised by them when completed. Even an attempt of this kind will rouse your powers.

But as mere enthusiasm will carry you but a little way, let me recommend a practice that may be equivalent, and will perhaps more efficaciously contribute to your advancement, than even the verbal corrections of those masters themselves, could they be obtained. What I would propose is, that you should enter into a kind of competition, by painting a similar subject, and making a companion to any picture that you consider as a model. After you have finished your work, place it near the model, and compare them carefully together. You will then not only see, but feel your own deficiencies more sensibly than by precepts, or any other means of instruction. The true principles of painting will mingle with your thoughts. Ideas thus fixed by sensible objects, will be certain and definitive; and sinking deep into the mind, will not only be more just, but more lasting than those presented to you by precepts only: which will, always be fleeting, variable, and undetermined.

This method of comparing your own efforts with those of some great master, is indeed a severe and mortifying task, to which none will submit, but such as have great views, with fortitude sufficient to forego the gratifications of present vanity for future honour. When the student has succeeded in some measure to his own satisfaction, and has felicitated himself on his success, to go voluntarily to a tribunal where he knows his vanity must be humbled, and all self-approbation must vanish, requires not only great resolution, but great humility. To him, however, who has the Ambition to be a real master, the solid satisfaction which proceeds from a consciousness of his advancement (of which seeing his own faults is the first step) will very abundantly compensate for the mortification of present disappointment. There is, besides, this alleviating circumstance. Every discovery he makes, every acquisition of knowledge he attains, seems to proceed from his own sagacity; and thus he acquires a confidence in himself sufficient to keep up the resolution of perseverance.

SECOND DISCOURSE

We all must have experienced how lazily, and consequently how ineffectually, instruction is received when forced upon the mind by others. Few have been taught to any purpose who have not been their own teachers. We prefer those instructions which we have given ourselves, from our affection to the instructor; and they are more effectual, from being received into the mind at the very time when it is most open and eager to receive them.

With respect to the pictures that you are to choose for your models, I could wish that you would take the world's opinion rather than your own. In other words, I would have you choose those of established reputation rather than follow your own fancy. If you should not admire them at first, you will, by endeavouring to imitate them, find that the world has not been mistaken.

It is not an easy task to point out those various excellences for your imitation which he distributed amongst the various schools. An endeavour to do this may perhaps be the subject of some future discourse. I will, therefore, at present only recommend a model for style in painting, which is a branch of the art more immediately necessary to the young student. Style in painting is the same as in writing, a power over materials, whether words or colours, by which conceptions or sentiments are conveyed. And in this Lodovico Carrache (I mean in his best works) appears to me to approach the nearest to perfection. His unaffected breadth of light and shadow, the simplicity of colouring, which holding its proper rank, does not draw aside the least part of the attention from the subject, and the solemn effect of that twilight which seems diffused over his pictures, appear to me to correspond with grave and dignified subjects, better than the more artificial brilliancy of sunshine which enlightens the pictures of Titian. Though Tintoret thought that Titian's colouring was the model of perfection, and would correspond even with the sublime of Michael Angelo; and that if Angelo had coloured like Titian, or Titian designed like Angelo, the world would once have had a perfect painter.

It is our misfortune, however, that those works of Carrache which I would recommend to the student are not often found out of Bologna. The "St. Francis in the midst of his Friars," "The Transfiguration," "The Birth of St. John the Baptist," "The Calling of St. Matthew," the "St. Jerome," the fresco paintings in the Zampieri Palace, are all worthy the attention of the student. And I think those who travel would do

35

well to allot a much greater portion of their time to that city than it has been hitherto the custom to bestow.

In this art, as in others, there are many teachers who profess to show the nearest way to excellence, and many expedients have been invented by which the toil of study might be saved. But let no man be seduced to idleness by specious promises. Excellence is never granted to man but as the reward of labour. It argues, indeed, no small strength of mind to persevere in habits of industry, without the pleasure of perceiving those advances; which, like the hand of a clock, whilst they make hourly approaches to their point, yet proceed so slowly as to escape observation. A facility of drawing, like that of playing upon a musical instrument, cannot be acquired but by an infinite number of acts. I need not, therefore, enforce by many words the necessity of continual application; nor tell you that the port-crayon ought to be for ever in your hands. Various methods will occur to you by which this power may be acquired. I would particularly recommend that after your return from the academy (where I suppose your attendance to be constant) you would endeavour to draw the figure by memory. I will even venture to add, that by perseverance in this custom, you will become able to draw the human figure tolerably correct, with as little effort of the mind as to trace with a pen the letters of the alphabet.

That this facility is not unattainable, some members in this academy give a sufficient proof. And, be assured, that if this power is not acquired whilst you are young, there will be no time for it afterwards: at least, the attempt will be attended with as much difficulty as those experience who learn to read or write after they have arrived to the age of maturity.

But while I mention the port-crayon as the student's constant companion, he must still remember that the pencil is the instrument by which he must hope to obtain eminence. What, therefore, I wish to impress upon you is, that whenever an opportunity offers, you paint your studies instead of drawing them. This will give you such a facility in using colours, that in time they will arrange themselves under the pencil, even without the attention of the hand that conducts it. If one act excluded the other, this advice could not with any propriety be given. But if painting comprises both drawing and colouring and if by a short struggle of resolute industry the same expedition is attainable in painting as in drawing on paper, I cannot see what objection can justly be made to the practice; or why that should be done by parts, which may be done altogether.

If we turn our eyes to the several schools of painting, and consider their respective excellences, we shall find that those who excel most in colouring pursued this method. The Venetian and Flemish schools, which owe much of their fame to colouring, have enriched the cabinets of the collectors of drawings with very few examples. Those of Titian, Paul Veronese, Tintoret, and the Bassans, are in general slight and undetermined. Their sketches on paper are as rude as their pictures are excellent in regard to harmony of colouring. Correggio and Barocci have left few, if any, finished drawings behind them. And in the Flemish school, Rubens and Vandyke made their designs for the most part either in colours or in chiaroscuro. It is as common to find studies of the Venetian and Flemish painters on canvas, as of the schools of Rome and Florence on paper. Not but that many finished drawings are sold under the names of those masters. Those, however, are undoubtedly the productions either of engravers or of their scholars who copied their works.

These instructions I have ventured to offer from my own experience; but as they deviate widely from received opinions, I offer them with diffidence; and when better are suggested, shall retract them without regret.

There is one precept, however, in which I shall only be opposed by the vain, the ignorant, and the idle. I am not afraid that I shall repeat it too often. You must have no dependence on your own genius. If you have great talents, industry will improve them: if you have but moderate abilities, industry will supply their deficiency. Nothing is denied to well-directed labour: nothing is to be obtained without it. Not to enter into metaphysical discussions on the nature or essence of genius, I will venture to assert, that assiduity unabated by difficulty, and a disposition eagerly directed to the object of its pursuit, will produce effects similar to those which some call the result of natural powers.

Though a man cannot at all times, and in all places, paint or draw, yet the mind can prepare itself by laying in proper materials, at all times, and in all places. Both Livy and Plutarch, in describing Philopoemen, one of the ablest generals of antiquity, have given us a striking picture of a mind always intent on its profession, and by assiduity obtaining those excellences which some all their lives vainly expect from Nature. I shall quote the passage in Livy at length, as it runs parallel with the practice I would recommend to the painter, sculptor, or architect.

"Philopoemen was a man eminent for his sagacity and experience in choosing ground, and in leading armies; to which he formed his mind by perpetual meditation, in times of peace as well as war. When, in any occasional journey, he came to a straight difficult passage, if he was alone, he considered with himself, and if he was in company he asked his friends what it would be best to do if in this place they had found an enemy, either in the front, or in the rear, on the one side, or on the other. 'It might happen,' says he, 'that the enemy to be opposed might come on drawn up in regular lines, or in a tumultuous body, formed only by the nature of the place.' He then considered a little what ground he should take; what number of soldiers he should use, and what arms he should give them; where he should lodge his carriages, his baggage, and the defenceless followers of his camp; how many guards, and of what kind, he should send to defend them; and whether it would be better to press forward along the pass, or recover by retreat his former station: he would consider likewise where his camp could most commodiously be formed; how much ground he should enclose within his trenches; where he should have the convenience of water; and where he might find plenty of wood and forage; and when he should break up his camp on the following day, through what road he could most safely pass, and in what form he should dispose his troops. With such thoughts and disquisitions he had from his early years so exercised his mind, that on these occasions nothing could happen which he had not been already accustomed to consider."

I cannot help imagining that I see a promising young painter, equally vigilant, whether at home, or abroad in the streets, or in the fields. Every object that presents itself is to him a lesson. He regards all nature with a view to his profession; and combines her beauties, or corrects her defects. He examines the countenance of men under the influence of passion; and often catches the most pleasing hints from subjects of turbulence or deformity. Even bad pictures themselves supply him with useful documents; and, as Leonardo da Vinci has observed, he improves upon the fanciful images that are sometimes seen in the fire, or are accidentally sketched upon a discoloured wall.

The artist who has his mind thus filled with ideas, and his hand made expert by practice, works with ease and readiness; whilst he who would have you believe that he is waiting for the inspirations of genius, is in reality at a loss how to beam, and is at last delivered of his monsters with difficulty and pain.

The well-grounded painter, on the contrary, has only maturely to consider his subject, and all the mechanical parts of his art follow without his exertion, Conscious of the difficulty of obtaining what he possesses he makes no pretensions to secrets, except those of closer application. Without conceiving the smallest jealousy against others, he is contented that all shall be as great as himself who are willing to undergo the same fatigue: and as his pre-eminence depends not upon a trick, he is free from the painful suspicions of a juggler, who lives in perpetual fear lest his trick should be discovered.

Joshua Reynolds
Kitty Fisher as Cleopatra Dissolving the Pearl
1759
oil on canvas, 76 x 63 cm
English Heritage, Kenwood

Joshua Reynolds
Lady Anstruther
circa 1763
oil on canvas, 76 x 62 cm
Manchester City Galleries

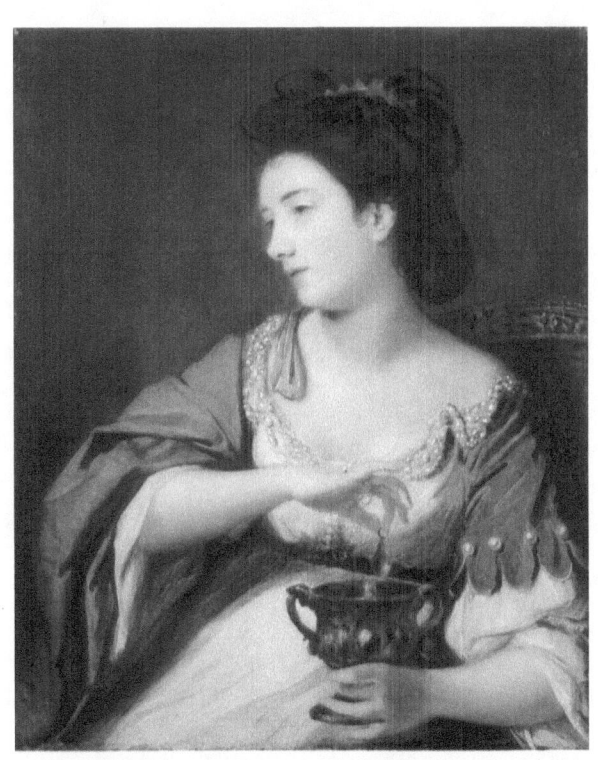

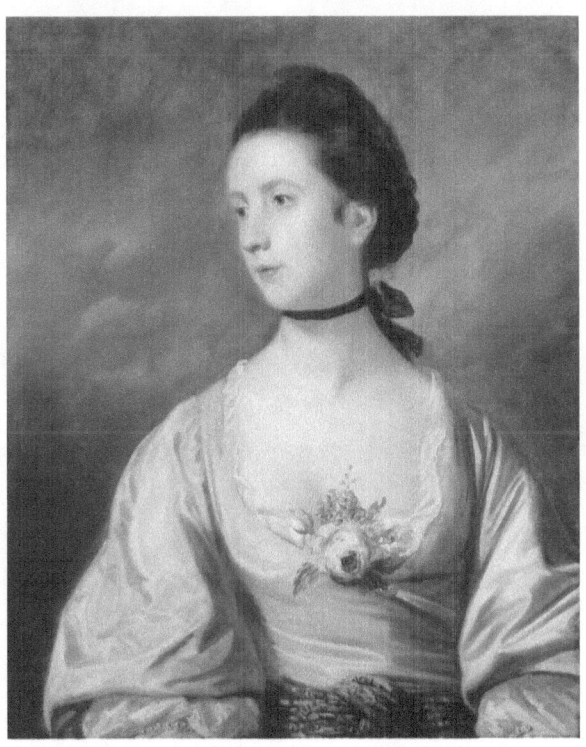

◇◇◇◇◇◇◇◇◇◇◇◇◇◇◇

DISCOURSE III

**Delivered to the Students of the Royal Academy
on the Distribution of the Prizes
December, 14, 1770
by the President**

G entlemen, — It is not easy to speak with propriety to so many
students of different ages and different degrees of advancement.
The mind requires nourishment adapted to its growth; and what
may have promoted our earlier efforts, might, retard us in our nearer
approaches to perfection.

The first endeavours of a young painter, as I have remarked in a
former discourse, must be employed in the attainment of mechanical
dexterity, and confined to the mere imitation of the object before him.
Those who have advanced beyond the rudiments, may, perhaps, find
advantage in reflecting on the advice which I have likewise given them,
when I recommended the diligent study of the works of our great predecessors; but I at the same time endeavoured to guard them against
an implicit submission to the authority of any one master, however
excellent; or by a strict imitation of his manner, to preclude ourselves
from the abundance and variety of nature. I will now add that nature
herself is not to be too closely copied. There are excellences in the art
of painting, beyond what is commonly called the imitation of nature:
and these excellences I wish to point out. The students who, having
passed through the initiatory exercises, are more advanced in the art,
and who, sure of their hand, have leisure to exert their understanding, must now be told that a mere copier of nature can never produce
anything great; can never raise and enlarge the conceptions, or warm
the heart of the spectator.

The wish of the genuine painter must be more extensive: instead
of endeavouring to amuse mankind with the minute neatness of his
imitations, he must endeavour to improve them by the grandeur of his
ideas; instead of seeking praise, by deceiving the superficial sense of
the spectator, he must strive for fame, by captivating the imagination.

The principle now laid down, that the perfection of this art does
not consist in mere imitation, is far from being new or singular. It is,

indeed, supported by the general opinion of the enlightened part of mankind. The poets, orators, and rhetoricians of antiquity, are continually enforcing this position, that all the arts receive their perfection from an ideal beauty, superior to what is to be found in individual nature. They are ever referring to the practice of the painters and sculptors of their times, particularly Phidias (the favourite artist of antiquity), to illustrate their assertions. As if they could not sufficiently express their admiration of his genius by what they knew, they have recourse to poetical enthusiasm. They call it inspiration; a gift from heaven. The artist is supposed to have ascended the celestial regions, to furnish his mind with this perfect idea of beauty. "He," says Proclus, "who takes for his model such forms as nature produces, and confines himself to an exact imitation of them, will never attain to what is perfectly beautiful. For the works of nature are full of disproportion, and fall very short of the true standard of beauty. So that Phidias, when he formed his Jupiter, did not copy any object ever presents to his sight; but contemplated only that image which he had conceived in his mind from Homer's description." And thus Cicero, speaking of the same Phidias: "Neither did this artist," says he, "when he carved the image of Jupiter or Minerva, set before him any one human figure as a pattern, which he was to copy; but having a more perfect idea of beauty fixed in his mind, this he steadily contemplated, and to the imitation of this all his skill and labour were directed."

The moderns are not less convinced than the ancients of this superior power existing in the art; nor less conscious of its effects. Every language has adopted terms expressive of this excellence. The *Gusto grande* of the Italians; the *Beau ideal* of the French and the *great style*, *genius*, and *taste* among the English, are but different appellations of the same thing. It is this intellectual dignity, they say, that ennobles the painter's art; that lays the line between him and the mere mechanic; and produces those great effects in an instant, which eloquence and poetry, by slow and repeated efforts, are scarcely able to attain.

Such is the warmth with which both the ancients and moderns speak of this divine principle of the art; but, as I have formerly observed, enthusiastic admiration seldom promotes knowledge. Though a student by such praise may have his attention roused, and a desire excited, of running in this great career, yet it is possible that what has been said to excite, may only serve to deter him. He examines his own mind, and perceives there nothing of that divine inspiration with which he is told so many others have been favoured. He never travelled to heaven to gather new ideas; and he finds himself possessed of no other qualifications than what mere common observation and a plain understanding can confer. Thus he becomes gloomy amidst the splendour of figurative declamation, and thinks it hopeless to pursue an object which he supposes out of the reach of human industry.

But on this, as upon many other occasions, we ought to distinguish how much is to be given to enthusiasm, and how much to reason. We ought to allow for, and we ought to commend, that strength of vivid expression which is necessary to convey, in its full force, the highest sense of the most complete effect of art; taking care at the same time not to lose in terms of vague admiration that solidity and truth of principle upon which alone we can reason, and may be enabled to practise.

It is not easy to define in what this great style consists; nor to describe, by words, the proper means of acquiring it, if the mind of the student should be at all capable of such an acquisition. Could we teach taste or genius by rules, they would be no longer taste and genius. But though there neither are, nor can be, any precise invariable rules for the exercise or the acquisition of those great qualities, yet we may as truly say that they always operate in proportion to our attention in observing the works of nature, to our skill in selecting, and to our care in digesting, methodising, and comparing our observations. There are many beauties in our art, that seem, at first, to lie without the reach of precept, and yet may easily be reduced to practical principles. Experience is all in all; but it is not every one who profits by experience; and most people err, not so much from want of capacity to find their object, as from not knowing what object to pursue. This great ideal perfection and beauty are not to be sought in the heavens, but upon the earth. They are about us, and upon every side of us. But the power of discovering what is deformed in nature, or in other words, what is particular and uncommon, can be acquired only by experience; and the whole beauty and grandeur of the art consists, in my opinion, in being able to get above all singular forms, local customs, particularities, and details of every kind.

All the objects which are exhibited to our view by nature, upon close examination will be found to have their blemishes and defects. The most beautiful forms have something about them like weakness, minuteness, or imperfection. But it is not every eye that perceives these blemishes. It must be an eye long used to the contemplation and comparison of these forms; and which, by a long habit of observing what any set of objects of the same kind have in common, that alone can acquire the power of discerning what each wants in particular. This long laborious comparison should be the first study of the painter who aims at the greatest style. By this means, he acquires a just idea of beautiful forms; he corrects nature by herself, her imperfect state by her more perfect. His eye being enabled to distinguish the accidental deficiencies, excrescences, and deformities of things from their general figures, he makes out an abstract idea of their forms more perfect than any one original; and what may seem a paradox, he learns to design naturally by drawing his figures unlike to any one object. This idea of the perfect state of nature, which the artist calls the ideal beauty, is the great leading principle by which works of genius are conducted. By this Phidias acquired his fame. He wrought upon a sober principle what has so much excited the enthusiasm of the world; and by this method you, who have courage to tread the same path, may acquire equal reputation.

This is the idea which has acquired, and which seems to have a right to the epithet of Divine; as it may be said to preside, like a supreme judge, over all the productions of nature; appearing to be possessed of the will and intention of the Creator, as far as they regard the external form of living beings.

When a man once possesses this idea in its perfection, there is no danger but that he will he sufficiently warmed by it himself, and be able to warm and ravish every one else.

Thus it is from a reiterated experience, and a close comparison of the objects in nature, that an artist becomes possessed of the idea of that central form, if I may so express it, from which every deviation is deformity. But the investigation of this form I grant is painful, and I know but of one method of shortening the road; this is, by a careful study of the works of the ancient sculptors; who, being indefatigable in the school of nature, have left models of that perfect form behind them, which an artist would prefer as supremely beautiful, who had spent his whole life in that single contemplation. But if industry carried them thus far, may not you also hope for the same reward from the same labour? We have the same school opened to us that was opened to them; for nature denies her instructions to none who desire to become her pupils.

To the principle I have laid down, that the idea of beauty in each species of beings is invariably one, it may be objected that in every particular species there are various central forms, which are separate and distinct from each other, and yet are undeniably beautiful; that in the human figure, for instance, the beauty of the Hercules is one, of the gladiator another, of the Apollo another, which makes so many different ideas of beauty.

It is true, indeed, that these figures are each perfect in their kind, though of different characters and proportions; but still none of them is the representation of an individual, but of a class. And as there is one general form, which, as I have said, belongs to the human kind at large, so in each of these classes there is one common idea and central form, which is the abstract of the various individual forms belonging to that class. Thus, though the forms of childhood and age differ exceedingly, there is a common form in childhood, and a common form in age,—which is the more perfect, as it is more remote from all peculiarities. But I must add further, that though the most perfect forms of each of the general divisions of the human figure are ideal, and superior to any individual form of that class, yet the highest perfection of the human figure is not to be found in any one of them. It is not in the Hercules, nor in the gladiator, nor in the Apollo; but in that form which is taken from them all, and which partakes equally of the activity of the gladiator, of the delicacy of the Apollo, and of the muscular strength of the Hercules. For perfect beauty in any species must combine all the characters which are beautiful in that species. It cannot consist in any one to the exclusion of the rest: no one, therefore, must be predominant, that no one may be deficient.

The knowledge of these different characters, and the power of separating and distinguishing them, is undoubtedly necessary to the painter, who is to vary his compositions with figures of various forms and proportions, though he is never to lose sight of the general idea of perfection in each kind.

There is, likewise, a kind of symmetry or proportion, which may properly be said to belong to deformity. A figure lean or corpulent, tall or short, though deviating from beauty, may still have a certain union of the various parts, which may contribute to make them, on the whole, not unpleasing. When the artist has by diligent attention acquired a clear and distinct idea of beauty and symmetry; when he has reduced the variety of nature to the abstract idea; his next task will be to become acquainted with the genuine habits of nature, as distinguished from those of fashion. For in the same manner, and on the same principles, as he has acquired the knowledge of the real forms of nature, distinct from accidental deformity, he must endeavour to separate simple chaste nature from those adventitious, those affected and forced airs or actions, with which she is loaded by modern education.

Perhaps I cannot better explain what I mean than by reminding you of what was taught us by the Professor of Anatomy, in respect to the natural position and movement of the feet. He observed that the fashion of turning, them outwards was contrary to the intent of nature, as might be seen from the structure of the bones, and from the weakness that proceeded from that manner of standing. To this we may add the erect position of the head, the projection of the chest, the walking with straight knees, and many such actions, which are merely the result of fashion, and what nature never warranted, as we are sure that we have been taught them when children.

I have mentioned but a few of those instances, in which vanity or caprice have contrived to distort and disfigure the human form; your own recollection will add to these a thousand more of ill-understood methods, that have been practised to disguise nature, among our dancing-masters, hair-dressers, and tailors, in their various schools of deformity.

However the mechanic and ornamental arts may sacrifice to fashion, she must be entirely excluded from the art of painting; the painter must never mistake this capricious changeling for the genuine offspring of nature; he must divest himself of all prejudices in favour of his age or country; he must disregard all local and temporary ornaments, and look only on those general habits that are everywhere and always the same. He addresses his works to the people of every country and every age; he calls upon posterity to be his spectators, and says with Zeuxis, *In æternitatem pingo.*

The neglect of separating modern fashions from the habits of nature, leads to that ridiculous style which has been practised by some painters who have given to Grecian heroes the airs and graces practised in the court of Louis XIV.; an absurdity almost as great as it would have been to have dressed them after the fashion of that court.

To avoid this error, however, and to retain the true simplicity of nature, is a task more difficult than at first sight it may appear. The prejudices in favour of the fashions and customs that we have been used to, and which are justly called a second nature, make it too often difficult to distinguish that which is natural from that which is the result of education; they frequently even give a predilection in favour of the artificial mode; and almost every one is apt to be guided by those local prejudices who has not chastised his mind, and regulated the instability of his affections, by the eternal invariable idea of nature.

Here, then, as before, we must have recourse to the ancients as instructors. It is from a careful study of their works that you will be enabled to attain to the real simplicity of nature; they will suggest many observations, which would probably escape you, if your study were confined to nature alone. And, indeed, I cannot help suspecting, that in this instance the ancients had an easier task than the moderns. They had, probably, little or nothing to unlearn, as their manners were nearly approaching to this desirable simplicity; while the modern artist, before he can see the truth of things, is obliged to remove a veil, with which the fashion of the times has thought proper to cover her.

Having gone thus far in our investigation of the great style in painting; if we now should suppose that the artist has formed the true idea of beauty, which enables him to give his works a correct and perfect design; if we should suppose also that he has acquired a knowledge of the unadulterated habits of nature, which gives him simplicity; the rest of his talk is, perhaps, less than is generally imagined. Beauty and simplicity have so great a share in the composition of a great style, that he who has acquired them has little else to learn. It must not, indeed, be forgot that there is a nobleness of conception, which goes beyond anything in the mere exhibition, even of perfect form; there is an art of animating and dignifying the figures with intellectual grandeur, of impressing the appearance of philosophic wisdom or heroic virtue. This can only be acquired by him that enlarges the sphere of his understanding by a variety of knowledge, and warms his imagination with the best productions of ancient and modern poetry.

A hand thus exercised, and a mind thus instructed, will bring the art to a higher degree of excellence than, perhaps, it has hitherto attained in this country. Such a student will disdain the humbler walks of painting, which, however profitable, can never assure him a permanent reputation. He will leave the meaner artist servilely to suppose that those are the best pictures which are most likely to deceive the spectator. He will permit the lower painter, like the florist or collector of shells, to exhibit the minute discriminations which distinguish one object of the same species from another; while he, like the philosopher, will consider nature in the abstract, and represent in every one of his figures the character of its species.

If deceiving the eye were the only business of the art, there is no doubt, indeed, but the minute painter would be more apt to succeed: but it is not the eye, it is the mind, which the painter of genius desires to address; nor will he waste a moment upon these smaller objects, which only serve to catch the sense, to divide the attention, and to counteract his great design of speaking to the heart.

This is the ambition I could wish to excite in your minds; and the object I have had in my view, throughout this discourse, is that one great idea which gives to painting its true dignity, that entitles it to the name of a Liberal Art, and ranks it as a sister of poetry.

It may possibly have happened to many young students whose application was sufficient to overcome all difficulties, and whose minds were capable of embracing the most extensive views, that they have, by a wrong direction originally given, spent their lives in the meaner walks of painting, without ever knowing there was a nobler to pursue. "Albert Durer," as Vasari has justly remarked, "would probably have been one of the first painters of his age (and he lived in an era of great artists) had he been initiated into those great principles of the art which were so well understood and practised by his contemporaries in Italy. But unluckily, having never seen or heard of any other manner, he considered his own, without doubt, as perfect."

As for the various departments of painting, which do not presume to make such high pretensions, they are many. None of them are without their merit, though none enter into competition with this great universal presiding idea of the art. The painters who have applied themselves more particularly to low and vulgar characters, and who express with precision the various shades of passion, as they are exhibited by vulgar minds (such as we see in the works of Hogarth) deserve great praise; but as their genius has been employed on low and confined subjects, the praise that we give must be as limited as its object.

The merrymaking or quarrelling of the Boors of Teniers; the same sort of productions of Brouwer, or Ostade, are excellent in their kind; and the excellence and its praise will be in proportion, as, in those limited subjects and peculiar forms, they introduce more or less of the expression of those passions, as they appear in general and more enlarged nature. This principle may be applied to the battle pieces of Bourgognone, the French gallantries of Watteau, and even beyond the exhibition of animal life, to the landscapes of Claude Lorraine, and the sea-views of Vandervelde. All these painters have, in general, the same right, in different degrees, to the name of a painter, which a satirist, an epigrammatist, a sonnetteer, a writer of pastorals, or descriptive poetry, has to that of a poet.

In the same rank, and, perhaps, of not so great merit, is the cold painter of portraits. But his correct and just imitation of his object has its merit. Even the painter of still life, whose highest ambition is to give a minute representation of every part of those low objects, which he sets before him, deserves praise in proportion to his attainment; because no part of this excellent art, so much the ornament of polished life, is destitute of value and use. These, however, are by no means the views to which the mind of the student ought to be *primarily* directed. By aiming at better things, if from particular inclination, or from the taste of the time and place he lives in, or from necessity, or from failure in the highest attempts, he is obliged to descend lower; he will bring into the lower sphere of art a grandeur of composition and character that will raise and ennoble his works far above their natural rank.

A man is not weak, though he may not be able to wield the club of Hercules; nor does a man always practise that which he esteems the beat; but does that which he can best do. In moderate attempts, there are many walks open to the artist. But as the idea of beauty is of necessity but one, so there can be but one great mode of painting; the leading principle of which I have endeavoured to explain.

I should be sorry if what is here recommended should be at all understood to countenance a careless or indetermined manner of painting. For though the painter is to overlook the accidental discriminations of nature, he is to pronounce distinctly, and with precision, the general forms of things. A firm and determined outline is one of the characteristics of the great style in painting; and, let me add, that he who possesses the knowledge of the exact form, that every part of nature ought to have, will be fond of expressing that knowledge with correctness and precision in all his works.

To conclude: I have endeavoured to reduce the idea of beauty to general principles. And I had the pleasure to observe that the professor of painting proceeded in the same method, when he showed you that the artifice of contrast was founded but on one principle. And I am convinced that this is the only means of advancing science, of clearing the mind from a confused heap of contradictory observations, that do but perplex and puzzle the student when he compares them, or misguide him if he gives himself up to their authority; but bringing them under one general head can alone give rest and satisfaction to an inquisitive mind.

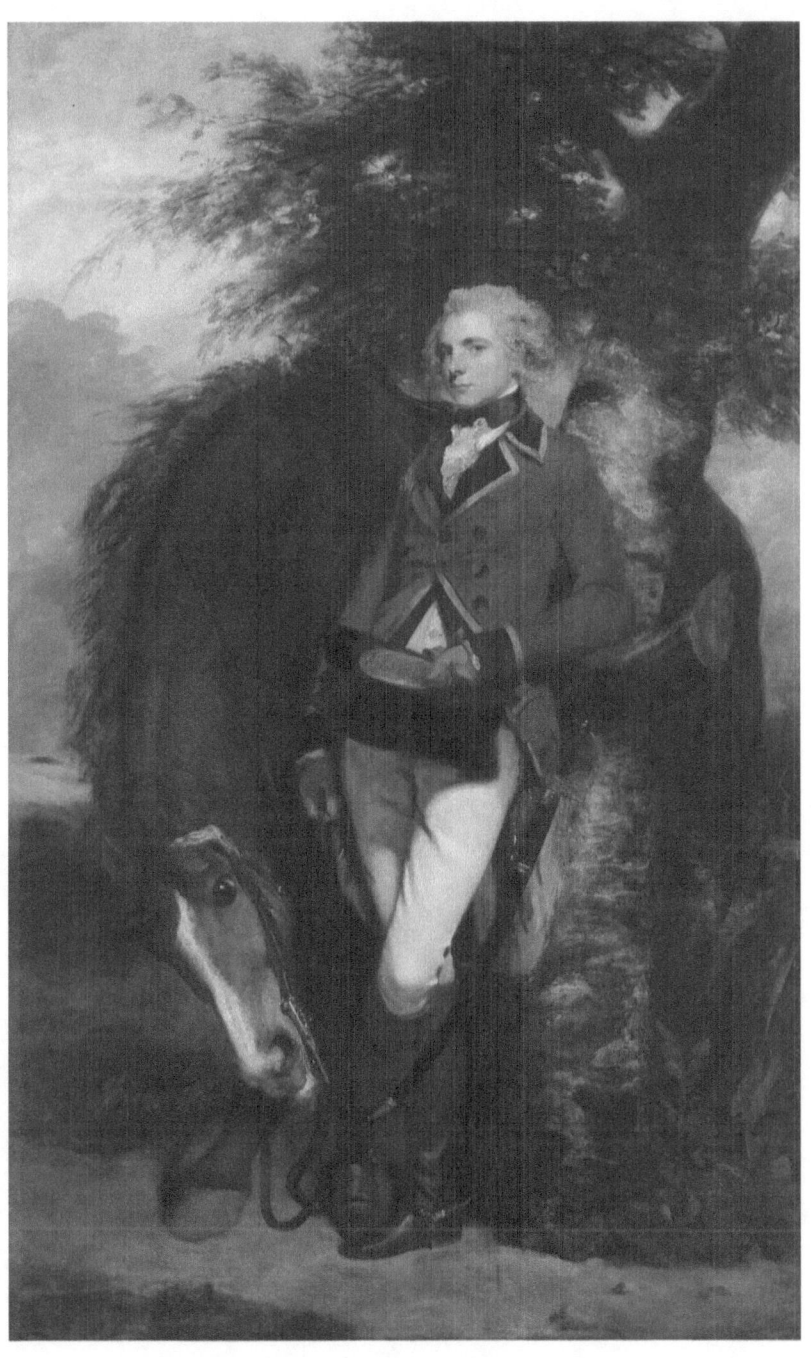

Joshua Reynolds
Colonel George K. H. Coussmaker
1782
oil on canvas, 238 x 145 cm
Metropolitan Museum of Art

◇◇◇◇◇◇◇◇◇◇◇◇◇◇

DISCOURSE IV

Delivered to the Students of the Royal Academy
on the Distribution of the Prizes
December 10, 1771
by the President.

Gentlemen, — The value and rank of every art is in proportion to the mental labour employed in it, or the mental pleasure produced by it. As this principle is observed or neglected, our profession becomes either a liberal art or a mechanical trade. In the hands of one man it makes the highest pretensions, as it is addressed to the noblest faculties, In those of another it is reduced to a mere matter of ornament, and the painter has but the humble province of furnishing our apartments with elegance.

This exertion of mind, which is the only circumstance that truly ennobles our art, makes the great distinction between the Roman and Venetian schools. I have formerly observed that perfect form is produced by leaving out particularities, and retaining only general ideas. I shall now endeavour to show that this principle, which I have proved to be metaphysically just, extends itself to every part of the art; that it gives what is called the grand style to invention, to composition, to expression, and even to colouring and drapery.

Invention in painting does not imply the invention of the subject, for that is commonly supplied by the poet or historian. With respect to the choice, no subject can be proper that is not generally interesting. It ought to be either some eminent instance of heroic action or heroic suffering. There must be something either in the action or in the object in which men are universally concerned, and which powerfully strikes upon the public sympathy.

Strictly speaking, indeed, no subject can be of universal, hardly can it be of general concern: but there are events and characters so popularly known in those countries where our art is in request, that they may be considered as sufficiently general for all our purposes. Such are the great events of Greek and Roman fable and history, which early education and the usual course of reading have made familiar and interesting to all Europe, without being degraded by the vulgarism of ordinary life in any country. Such, too, are the capital subjects of Scripture history, which, besides their general notoriety, become venerable by their connection with our religion.

As it is required that the subject selected should be a general one, it is no less necessary that it should be kept unembarrassed with whatever may any way serve to divide the attention of the spectator. Whenever a story is related, every man forms a picture in his mind of the action and the expression of the persons employed. The power of representing this mental picture in canvas is what we call invention in a painter. And as in the conception of this ideal picture the mind does not enter into the minute peculiarities of the dress, furniture, or scene of action, so when the painter comes to represent it he contrives those little necessary concomitant circumstances in such a manner that they shall strike the spectator no more than they did himself in his first conception of the story.

I am very ready to allow that some circumstances of minuteness and particularity frequently tend to give an air of truth to a piece, and to interest the spectator in an extraordinary manner. Such circumstances, therefore, cannot wholly be rejected; but if there be anything in the art which requires peculiar nicety of discernment, it is the disposition of these minute circumstantial parts which, according to the judgment employed in the choice, become so useful to truth or so injurious to grandeur.

However, the usual and most dangerous error is on the side of minuteness, and, therefore, I think caution most necessary where most have failed. The general idea constitutes real excellence. All smaller things, however perfect in their way, are to be sacrificed without mercy to the greater. The painter will not inquire what things may be admitted without much censure. He will not think it enough to show that they may be there; he will show that they must be there, that their absence would render his picture maimed and defective.

Thus, though to the principal group a second or third be added, and a second and third mass of light, care must be yet taken that these subordinate actions and lights, neither each in particular, nor all together, come into any degree of competition with the principal; they should make a part of that whole which would be imperfect without them. To every part of painting this rule may be applied. Even in portraits, the grace and, we may add, the likeness, consists more in taking the general air than in observing the effect similitude of every feature.

Thus figures must have a ground whereon to stand; they must be clothed, there must be a background, there must be light and shadow; but none of these ought to appear to have taken up any part of the artist's attention. They should be so managed as not even to catch that of the spectator. We know well enough, when we analyze a piece, the difficulty and the subtlety with which an artist adjusts the background, drapery, and masses of light; we know that a considerable part of the grace and effect of his picture depends upon them; but this art is so much concealed, even to a judicious eye, that no remains of any of these subordinate parts occur to memory when the picture is not present.

The great end of the art is to strike the imagination. The painter is, therefore, to make no ostentation of the means by which this is done; the spectator is only to feel the result in his bosom. An inferior artist is unwilling that any part of his industry should be lost upon the spectator. He takes as much pains to discover, as the greater artist does to conceal, the marks of his subordinate assiduity. In works of the lower kind everything appears studied and encumbered; it is all boastful art and open affectation. The ignorant often part from such pictures with wonder in their mouths, and indifference in their hearts.

But it is not enough in invention that the artist should restrain and keep under all the inferior parts of his subject; he must sometimes deviate from vulgar and strict historical truth in pursuing the grandeur of his design.

How much the great style exacts from its professors to conceive and represent their subjects in a poetical manner, not confined to mere matter of fact, may be seen in the cartoons of Raffaelle. In all the pictures in which the painter has represented the apostles, he has drawn them with great nobleness; he has given them as much dignity as the human figure is capable of receiving yet we are expressly told in Scripture they had no such respectable appearance; and of St. Paul in particular, we are told by himself, that his bodily presence was mean. Alexander is said to have been of a low stature: a painter ought not so to represent him. Agesilaus was low, lame, and of a mean appearance. None of these defects ought to appear in a piece of which he is the hero. In conformity to custom, I call this part of the art history painting; it ought to be called poetical, as in reality it is.

All this is not falsifying any fact; it is taking an allowed poetical licence. A painter of portraits retains the individual likeness; a painter of history shows the man by showing his actions. A painter must compensate the natural deficiencies of his art. He has but one sentence to utter, but one moment to exhibit. He cannot, like the poet or historian, expatiate, and impress the mind with great veneration for the character of the hero or saint he represents, though he lets us know at the same time that the saint was deformed, or the hero lame. The painter has no other means of giving an idea of the dignity of the mind, but by that external appearance which grandeur of thought does generally, though not always, impress on the countenance, and by that correspondence of figure to sentiment and situation which all men wish, but cannot command. The painter, who may in this one particular attain with ease what others desire in vain, ought to give all that he possibly can, since there are so many circumstances of true greatness that he cannot give at all. He cannot make his hero talk like a great man; he must make him look like one. For which reason he ought to be well studied in the analysis of those circumstances which constitute dignity of appearance in real life.

As in invention, so likewise in, expression, care must be taken not to run into particularities, Those expressions alone should be given to the figures which their respective situations generally produce. Nor is this enough; each person should also have that expression which men of his rank generally exhibit. The joy or the grief of a character of dignity is not to be expressed in the same manner as a similar passion in a vulgar face. Upon this principle Bernini, perhaps, may be subject to censure. This sculptor, in many respects admirable, has given a very mean expression to his statue of David, who is represented as just going to throw the stone from the sling; and in order to give it the expression of energy he has made him biting his under-lip. This expression is far from being general, and still farther from being dignified. He might have seen it in an instance or two, and he mistook accident for universality.

With respect to colouring, though it may appear at first a part of painting merely mechanical, yet it still has its rules, and those grounded upon that presiding principle which regulates both the great and the little in the study of a painter. By this, the first effect of the picture is produced; and as this is performed the spectator, as he walks the gallery, will stop, or pass along. To give a general air of grandeur at first view, all trifling or artful play of little lights or an attention to a variety of tints is to be avoided; a quietness and simplicity must reign over the whole work; to which a breadth of uniform and simple colour will very much contribute. Grandeur of effect is produced by two different ways, which seem entirely opposed to each other. One is, by reducing the colours to little more than chiaroscuro, which was often the practice of the Bolognian schools; and the other, by making the colours very distinct and forcible, such as we see in those of Rome and Florence; but still, the presiding principle of both those manners is simplicity. Certainly, nothing can be more simple than monotony, and the distinct blue, red, and yellow colours which are seen in the draperies of the Roman and Florentine schools, though they have not that kind of harmony which is produced by a variety of broken and transparent colours, have that effect of grandeur that was intended. Perhaps these distinct colours strike the mind more forcibly, from there not being any great union between them; as martial music, which is intended to rouse the noble passions, has its effect from the sudden and strongly marked transitions from one note to another, which that style of music requires; whilst in that which is intended to move the softer passions the notes imperceptibly melt into one another.

In the same manner as the historical painter never enters into the detail of colours, so neither does he debase his conceptions with minute attention to the discriminations of drapery. It is the inferior style that marks the variety of stuffs. With him, the clothing is neither woollen, nor linen, nor silk, satin, or velvet: it is drapery; it is nothing more. The art of disposing the foldings of the drapery make a very considerable part of the painter's study. To make it merely natural is a mechanical operation, to which neither genius or taste are required; whereas, it requires the nicest judgment to dispose the drapery, so that the folds have an easy communication, and gracefully follow each other, with such natural negligence as to look like the effect of chance, and at the same time show the figure under it to the utmost advantage.

Carlo Maratti was of opinion that the disposition of drapery was a more difficult art than even that of drawing the human figure; that a student might be more easily taught the latter than the former; as the rules of drapery, he said, could not be so well ascertained as those for delineating a correct form, This, perhaps, is a proof how willingly we favour our own peculiar excellence. Carlo Maratti is said to have valued himself particularly upon his skill in this part of the art yet in him the disposition appears so artificial, that he is inferior to Raffaelle, even in that which gave him his best claim to reputation.

Such is the great principle by which we must be directed in the nobler branches of our art. Upon this principle the Roman, the Florentine, the Bolognese schools, have formed their practice; and by this they have deservedly obtained the highest praise. These are the three great schools of the world in the epic style. The best of the French school, Poussin, Le Sueur, and Le Brun, have formed themselves upon these models, and consequently may be said, though Frenchmen, to be a colony from the Roman school. Next to these, but in a very different style of excellence, we may rank the Venetian, together with the Flemish and the Dutch schools, all professing to depart from the great purposes of painting, and catching at applause by inferior qualities.

I am not ignorant that some will censure me for placing the Venetians in this inferior class, and many of the warmest admirers of painting will think them unjustly degraded; but I wish not to be misunderstood. Though I can by no means allow them to hold any rank with the nobler schools of painting, they accomplished perfectly the thing they attempted. But as mere elegance is their principal object, as they seem more willing to dazzle than to affect, it can be no injury to them to suppose that their practice is useful only to its proper end. But what may heighten the elegant may degrade the sublime. There is a simplicity, and I may add, severity, in the great manner, which is, I am afraid, almost incompatible with this comparatively sensual style.

Tintoret, Paul Veronese, and others of the Venetian schools, seem to have painted with no other purpose than to be admired for their skill and expertness in the mechanism of painting, and to make a parade of that art which, as I before observed, the higher style requires its followers to conceal.

In a conference of the French Academy, at which were present Le Brun, Sebastian Bourdon, and all the eminent artists of that age, one of the academicians desired to have their opinion on the conduct of Paul Veronese, who, though a painter of great consideration, had, contrary to the strict rules of art, in his picture of Perseus and Andromeda, represented the principal figure in shade. To this question no satisfactory answer was then given. But I will venture to say, that if they had considered the class of the artist, and ranked him as an ornamental painter, there would have been no difficulty in answering: "It was unreasonable to expect what was never intended. His intention was solely to produce an effect of light and Shadow; everything was to be sacrificed to that intent, and the capricious composition of that picture suited very well with the style he professed."

Young minds are indeed too apt to be captivated by this splendour of style, and that of the Venetians will be particularly pleasing; for by them all those parts of the art that give pleasure to the eye or sense have been cultivated with care, and carried to the degree nearest to perfection. The powers exerted in the mechanical part of the art have been called the language of painters; but we must say, that it is but poor eloquence which only shows that the orator can talk. Words should be employed as the means, not as the end: language is the instrument, conviction is the work.

The language of painting must indeed be allowed these masters; but even in that they have shown more copiousness than choice, and more luxuriancy than judgment. If we consider the uninteresting subjects of their invention, or at least the uninteresting manner in which they are treated; if we attend to their capricious composition, their violent and affected contrasts, whether of figures, or of light and shadow, the richness of their drapery, and, at the same time, the mean effect which the discrimination of stuffs gives to their pictures; if to these we add their total inattention to expression, and then reflect on the conceptions and the learning of Michael Angelo, or the simplicity of Raffaelle, we can no longer dwell on the comparison. Even in colouring, if we compare the quietness and chastity of the Bolognese pencil to the bustle and tumult that fills every part of, a Venetian picture, without the least attempt to interest the passions, their boasted art will appear a mere struggle without effect; an empty tale told by an idiot, full of sound and fury, signifying nothing.

Such as suppose that the great style might happily be blended with the ornamental, that the simple, grave, and majestic dignity of Raffaelle could unite with the glow and bustle of a Paulo or Tintoret, are totally mistaken. The principles by which each are attained are so contrary to each other, that they seem, in my opinion, incompatible, and as impossible to exist together, as to unite in the mind at the same time the most sublime ideas and the lowest sensuality.

The subjects of the Venetian painters are mostly such as give them an opportunity of introducing a great number of figures, such as feasts, marriages, and processions, public martyrdoms, or miracles. I can easily conceive that Paul Veronese, if he were asked, would say that no subject was proper for an historical picture but such as admitted at least forty figures; for in a less number, he would assert, there could be no opportunity of the painter's showing his art in composition, his dexterity of managing and disposing the masses of light, and groups of figures, and of introducing a variety of Eastern dresses and characters in their rich stuffs.

But the thing is very different with a pupil of the greater schools. Annibale Caracci thought twelve figures sufficient for any story: he conceived that more would contribute to no end but to fill space; that they would, be but cold spectators of the general action, or, to use his own expression, that they would be figures to be let. Besides, it is impossible for a picture composed of so many parts to have that effect, so indispensably necessary to grandeur, of one complete whole. However contradictory it may be in geometry, it is true in taste, that many little things will not make a great one. The sublime impresses the mind at once with one great idea; it is a single blow: the elegant indeed may be produced by a repetition, by an accumulation of many minute circumstances.

However great the difference is between the composition of the Venetian and the rest of the Italian schools, there is full as great a disparity in the effect of their pictures as produced by colours. And though in this respect the Venetians must be allowed extraordinary skill, yet even that skill, as they have employed it, will but ill correspond with the great style. Their colouring is not only too brilliant, but, I will venture to say, too harmonious to produce that solidity, steadiness, and simplicity of effect which heroic subjects require, and which simple or grave colours only can give to a work. That they are to be cautiously studied by those who are ambitious of treading the great walk of history is confirmed, if it wants confirmation, by the greatest of all authorities, Michael Angelo. This wonderful man, after having seen a picture by Titian, told Vasari, who accompanied him, "that he liked much his colouring and manner; but then he added, that it was a pity the Venetian painters did not learn to draw correctly in their early youth, and adopt a better manner of study."

By this it appears that the principal attention of the Venetian painters, in the opinion of Michael Angelo, seemed to be engrossed by the study of colours, to the neglect of the ideal beauty of form, or propriety of expression. But if general censure was given to that school from the sight of a picture of Titian, how much more heavily, and more justly, would the censure fall on Paulo Veronese, or more especially on Tintoret? And here I cannot avoid citing Vasari's opinion of the style and manner of Tintoret. "Of all the extraordinary geniuses," says he, "that have ever practised the art of painting, for wild, capricious, extravagant, and fantastical inventions, for furious impetuosity and boldness in the execution of his work, there is none like Tintoret; his strange whims are even beyond extravagance; and his works seem to be produced rather by chance than in consequence of any previous design, as if he wanted to convince the world that, the art was a trifle, and of the most easy attainment."

For my own part, when I speak of the Venetian painters, I wish to be understood to mean Paulo Veronese and Tintoret, to the exclusion of Titian; for though his style is not so pure as that of many other of the Italian schools, yet there is a sort of senatorial dignity about him, which, however awkward in his imitators, seems to become him exceedingly. His portraits alone, from the nobleness and simplicity of character which he always gave them, will entitle him to the greatest respect, as he undoubtedly stands in the first rank in this branch of the art.

It is not with Titian, but with the seducing qualities of the two former, that I could wish to caution you, against being too much captivated. These are the persons who may be said to have exhausted all the powers of florid eloquence, to debauch the young and unexperienced, and have, without doubt, been the cause of turning off the attention of the connoisseur and of the patron of art, as well as that of the painter, from those higher excellences of which the art is capable, and which ought to be required in every considerable production. By them, and their imitators, a style merely ornamental has been disseminated throughout all Europe. Rubens carried it to Flanders, Voet to France, and Luca Giordano to Spain and Naples.

The Venetian is indeed the most splendid of the schools of elegance; and it is not without reason that the best performances in this lower school are valued higher than the second-rate performances of those above them; for every picture has value when it has a decided character, and is excellent in its kind. But the student must take care not to be so much dazzled with this splendour as to be tempted to imitate what must ultimately lead from perfection. Poussin, whose eye was always steadily fixed on the sublime, has been often heard to say, "That a particular attention to colouring was an obstacle to the student in his progress to the great end and design of the art; and that he who attaches himself to this principal end will acquire by practice a reasonably good method of colouring."

Though it be allowed that elaborate harmony of colouring, a brilliancy of tints, a soft and gradual transition from one to another, present to the eye what an harmonious concert of music does to the ear, it must be remembered that painting is not merely a gratification of the sight. Such excellence, though properly cultivated where nothing higher than elegance is intended, is weak and unworthy of regard, when the work aspires to grandeur and sublimity.

The same reasons that have been urged why a mixture of the Venetian style cannot improve the great style will hold good in regard to the Flemish and Dutch schools. Indeed, the Flemish school, of which Rubens is the head, was formed upon that of the Venetian; like them, he took his figures too much from the people before him. But it must be allowed in favour of the Venetians that he was more gross than they, and carried all their mistaken methods to a far greater excess. In the Venetian school itself, where they all err from the same cause, there is a difference in the effect. The difference between Paulo and Bassano seems to be only that one introduced Venetian gentlemen into his pictures, and the other the boors of the district of Bassano, and called them patriarchs and prophets.

The painters of the Dutch school have still more locality. With them, a history piece is properly a portrait of themselves; whether they describe the inside or outside of their houses, we have their own people engaged in their own peculiar occupations, working or drinking, playing or fighting. The circumstances that enter into a picture of this kind are so far from giving a general view of human life that they exhibit all the minute particularities of a nation differing in several respects from the rest of mankind. Yet, let them have their share of more humble praise. The painters of this school are excellent in their own way; they are only ridiculous when they attempt general history on their own narrow principles, and debase great events by the meanness of their characters.

Some inferior dexterity, some extraordinary mechanical power, is apparently that from which they seek distinction. Thus, we see, that school alone has the custom of representing candle-light, not as it really appears to us by night, but red, as it would illuminate objects to a spectator by day. Such tricks, however pardonable in the little style, where petty effects are the sole end, are inexcusable in the greater, where the attention should never be drawn aside by trifles, but should be entirely occupied by the subject itself.

The same local principles which characterise the Dutch school extend even to their landscape painters; and Rubens himself, who has painted many landscapes, has sometimes transgressed in this particular. Their pieces in this way are, I think, always a representation of an individual spot, and each in its kind a very faithful but very confined portrait.

Claude Lorraine, on the contrary, was convinced that taking nature as he found it seldom produced beauty. His pictures are a composition of the various draughts which he has previously made from various beautiful scenes and prospects. However, Rubens in some measure has made amends for the deficiency with which he is charged; he has contrived to raise and animate his otherwise uninteresting views, by introducing a rainbow, storm, or some particular accidental effect of light. That the practice of Claude Lorraine, in respect to his choice, is to be adopted by landscape painters, in opposition to that of the Flemish and Dutch schools, there can be no doubt, as its truth is founded upon the same principle as that by which the historical painter acquires perfect form. But whether landscape painting has a right to aspire so far as to reject what the painters call accidents of nature is not easy to determine. It is certain Claude Lorraine seldom, if ever, availed himself of those accidents; either he thought that such peculiarities were contrary to that style of general nature which he professed, or that it would catch the attention too strongly, and destroy that quietness and repose which he thought necessary to that kind of painting.

A portrait painter likewise, when he attempts history, unless he is upon his guard, is likely to enter too much into the detail. He too frequently makes his historical heads look like portraits; and this was once the custom amongst those old painters who revived the art before general ideas were practised or understood. A history painter paints man in general; a portrait painter, a particular man, and consequently a defective model.

Thus an habitual practice in the lower exercises of the art will prevent many from attaining the greater. But such of us who move in these humbler walks of the profession are not ignorant that, as the natural dignity of the subject is less, the more all the little ornamental helps are necessary to its embellishment. It would be ridiculous for a painter of domestic scenes, of portraits, landscapes, animals, or of still life, to say that he despised those qualities which have made the subordinate schools so famous. The art of colouring, and the skilful management of light and shadow, are essential requisites in his confined labours. If we descend still lower, what is the painter of fruit and flowers without the utmost art in colouring, and what the painters call handling; that is, a lightness of pencil that implies great practice, and gives the appearance of being done with ease? Some here, I believe, must remember a flower-painter whose boast it was that he scorned to paint for the million; no, he professed to paint in the true Italian taste; and despising the crowd, called strenuously upon the few to admire him. His idea of the Italian taste was to paint as black and dirty as he could, and to leave all clearness and brilliancy of colouring to those who were fonder of money than of immortality. The consequence was such as might be expected. For these pretty excellences are here essential beauties; and without this merit the artist's work will be more short-lived than the objects of his imitation.

From what has been advanced, we must now be convinced that there are two distinct styles in history painting: the grand, and the splendid or ornamental.

The great style stands alone, and does not require, perhaps does not so well admit, any addition from inferior beauties. The ornamental style also possesses its own peculiar merit. However, though the union of the two may make a sort of composite style, yet that style is likely to be more imperfect than either of those which go to its composition. Both kinds have merit, and may be excellent though in different ranks, if uniformity be preserved, and the general and particular ideas of nature be not mixed. Even the meanest of them is difficult enough to attain; and the first place being already occupied by the great artists in either department, some of those who followed thought there was less room for them, and feeling the impulse of ambition and the desire of novelty, and being at the same time perhaps willing to take the shortest way, they endeavoured to make for themselves a place between both. This they have effected by forming a union of the different orders. But as the grave and majestic style would suffer by a union with the florid and gay, so also has the Venetian ornament in some respect been injured by attempting an alliance with simplicity.

It may be asserted that the great style is always more or less contaminated by any meaner mixture. But it happens in a few instances that the lower may be improved by borrowing from the grand. Thus, if a portrait painter is desirous to raise and improve his subject, he has no other means than by approaching it to a general idea. He leaves out all the minute breaks and peculiarities in the face, and changes the dress from a temporary fashion to one more permanent, which has annexed to it no ideas of meanness from its being familiar to us. But if an exact resemblance of an individual be considered as the sole object to be aimed at, the portrait painter will be apt to lose more than he gains by the acquired dignity taken from general nature. It is very difficult to ennoble the character of a countenance but at the expense of the likeness, which is what is most generally required by such as sit to the painter.

Of those who have practised the composite style, and have succeeded in this perilous attempt, perhaps the foremost is Correggio. His style is founded upon modern grace and elegance, to which is super, added something of the simplicity of the grand style. A breadth of light and colour, the general ideas of the drapery, an uninterrupted flow of outline, all conspire to this effect. Next him (perhaps equal to him) Parmegiano has dignified the genteelness of modern effeminacy by uniting it with the simplicity of the ancients and the grandeur and severity of Michael Angelo. It must be confessed, however, that these two extraordinary men, by endeavouring to give the utmost degree of grace, have sometimes, perhaps, exceeded its boundaries, and have fallen into the most hateful of all hateful qualities, affectation. Indeed, it is the peculiar characteristic of men of genius to be afraid of coldness and insipidity, from which they think they never can be too far removed. It particularly happens to these great masters of grace and elegance. They often boldly drive on to the very verge of ridicule; the spectator is alarmed, but at the same time admires their vigour and intrepidity.

Strange graces still, and stranger flights they had,
. . .
Yet ne'er so sure our passion to create
Ae when they touch'd the brink of all we hate.

The errors of genius, however, are pardonable, and none even of the more exalted painters are wholly free from them; but they have taught us, by the rectitude of their general practice, to correct their own affected or accidental deviation. The very first have not been always upon their guard, and perhaps there is not a fault but what may take shelter under the most venerable authorities; yet that style only is perfect in which the noblest principles are uniformly pursued; and those masters only are entitled to the first rank in, our estimation who have enlarged the boundaries of their art, and have raised it to its highest dignity, by exhibiting the general ideas of nature.

On the whole, it seems to me that there is but one presiding principle which regulates and gives stability to every art. The works, whether of poets, painters, moralists, or historians, which are built upon general nature, live for ever; while those which depend for their existence on particular customs and habits, a partial view of nature, or the fluctuation of fashion, can only be coeval with that which first raised them from obscurity. Present time and future maybe considered as rivals, and he who solicits the one must expect to be discountenanced by the other.

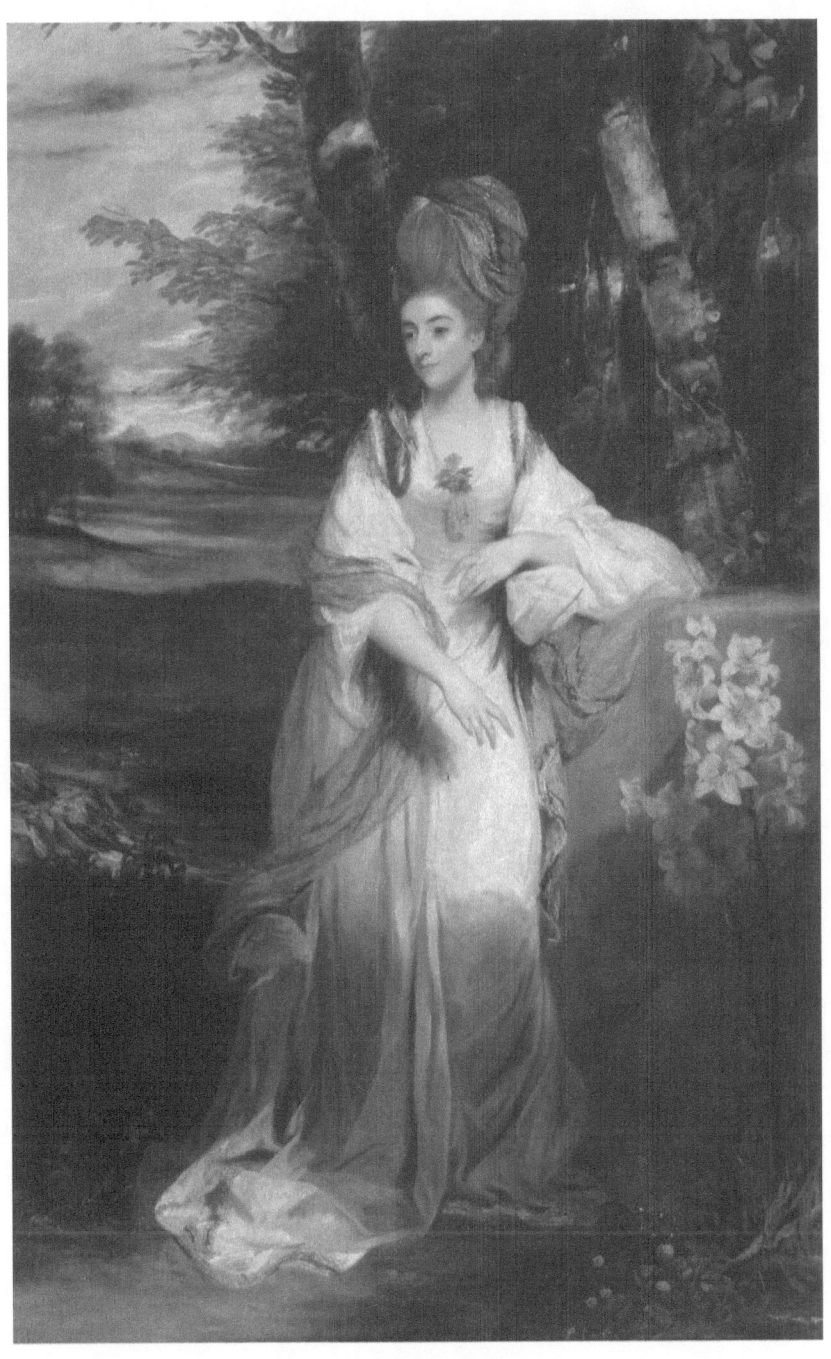

Joshua Reynolds
Lady Bampfylde
circa 1776
oil on canvas, 238 x 148 cm
Tate Britain

DISCOURSE V

**Delivered to the Students of the Royal Academy
on the Distribution of the Prizes
December 10, 1772
by the President**

G entlemen, — I purpose to carry on in this discourse the subject which I began in my last. It was my wish upon that occasion to incite you to pursue the higher excellences of the art. But I fear that in this particular I have been misunderstood. Some are ready to imagine, when any of their favourite acquirements in the art are properly classed, that they are utterly disgraced. This is a very great mistake: nothing has its proper lustre but in its proper place. That which is most worthy of esteem in its allotted sphere becomes an object, not of respect, but of derision, when it is forced into a higher, to which it is not suited; and there it becomes doubly a source of disorder, by occupying a situation which is not natural to it, and by putting down from the first place what is in reality of too much magnitude to become with grace and proportion that subordinate station, to which something of less value would be much better suited.

My advice in a word is this: keep your principal attention fixed upon the higher excellences. If you compass them and compass nothing more, you are still in the first class. We may regret the innumerable beauties which you may want: you may be very imperfect: but still, you are an imperfect person of the highest order.

If, when you have got thus far, you can add any, or all, of the subordinate qualifications, it is my wish and advice that you should not neglect them.

But this is as much a matter of circumspection and caution at least as of eagerness and pursuit.

The mind is apt to be distracted by a multiplicity of pursuits; and that scale of perfection, which I wish always to be preserved, is in the greatest danger of being totally disordered, and even inverted.

Some excellences bear to be united, and are improved by union, others are of a discordant nature; and the attempt to join them only produces a harsher jarring of incongruent principles.

The attempt to unite contrary excellences (of form, for instance) in a single figure, can never escape degenerating into the monstrous, but by sinking into the insipid, taking away its marked character, and weakening its expression.

This remark is true to a certain degree with regard to the passions. If you mean to preserve the most perfect beauty in its most perfect state, you cannot express the passions, which produce (all of them) distortion and deformity, more or less, in the most beautiful faces.

Guido, from want of choice in adapting his subject to his ideas and his powers, or in attempting to preserve beauty where it could not be preserved has in this respect succeeded very ill. His figures are often engaged in subjects that required great expression: yet his "Judith and Holofernes," the "Daughter of Herodias with the Baptist's Head," the "Andromeda," and even the "Mothers of the Innocents," have little more expression than his "Venus attired by the Graces."

Obvious as these remarks appear, there are many writers on our art, who, not being of the profession, and consequently not knowing what can or what cannot be done, have been very liberal of absurd praises in their descriptions of favourite works. They always find in them what they are resolved to find. They praise excellences that can hardly exist together, and above all things are fond of describing with great exactness the expression of a mixed passion, which more par-ticularly appears to me out of the reach of our art.

Such are many disquisitions which I have read on some of the car-toons and other pictures of Raffaelle, where the critics have described their own imagination; or indeed where the excellent master himself may have attempted this expression of passions above the powers of the art; and has, therefore, by an indistinct and imperfect marking, left room for every imagination, with equal probability to find a pas-sion of his own. What has been, and what can be done in the art, is sufficiently difficult; we need not be mortified or discouraged for not being able to execute the conceptions of a romantic imagination. Art has its boundaries, though imagination has none. We can easily, like the ancients, suppose a Jupiter to be possessed of all those powers and perfections which the subordinate Deities were endowed with separately. Yet, when they employed their art to represent him, they confined his character to majesty alone. Pliny, therefore, though we are under great obligations to him for the information he has given us in relation to the works of the ancient artists, is very frequently wrong when he speaks of them, which he does very often in the style of many of our modern connoisseurs. He observes that in a statue of Paris, by Fuphranor, you might discover at the same time three different characters; the dignity of a judge of the goddesses, the lover of Helen, and the conqueror of Achilles. A statue in which you endeavour to unite stately dignity, youthful elegance, and stern valour, must surely possess none of these to any eminent degree.

From hence it appears that there is much difficulty as well as danger in an endeavour to concentrate upon a single subject those various powers which, rising from different points, naturally move in different directions.

The summit of excellence seems to be an assemblage of contrary qualities, but mixed, in such proportions, that no one part is found to counteract the other. How hard this is to be attained in every art, those only know who have made the greatest progress in their respective professions.

To conclude what I have to say on this part of the subject, which I think of great importance, I wish you to understand that I do not discourage the younger students from the noble attempt of uniting all the excellences of art, but to make them aware that, besides the difficulties which attend every arduous attempt, there is a peculiar difficulty in the choice of the excellences which ought to be united; I wish you to attend to this, that you may try yourselves, whenever you are capable of that trial, what you can, and what you cannot do: and that, instead of dissipating your natural faculties over the immense field of possible excellence, you may choose some particular walk in which you may exercise all your powers, in order each of you to be the first in his way. If any man shall be master of such a transcendent, commanding, and ductile genius, as to enable him to rise to the highest, and to stoop to the lowest flights of art, and to sweep over all of them unobstructed and secure, he is fitter to give example than to receive instruction.

Having said thus much on the union of excellences, I will next say something of the subordination in which various excellences ought to be kept.

I am of opinion that the ornamental style, which in my discourse of last year I cautioned you against considering as principal, may not be wholly unworthy the attention of those who aim even at the grand style; when it is properly placed and properly reduced.

But this study will be used with far better effect, if its principles are employed in softening the harshness and mitigating the rigour of the great style, than if in attempt to stand forward with any pretensions of its own to positive and original excellence.

It was thus Lodovico Caracci, whose example I formerly recommended to you, employed it. He was acquainted with the works both of Correggio and the Venetian painters, and knew the principles by which they produced those pleasing effects which at the first glance prepossess us so much in their favour; but he took only as much from each as would embellish, but not overpower, that manly strength and energy of style, which is his peculiar character.

Since I have already expatiated so largely in my former discourse, and in my present, upon the styles and characters of painting, it will not be at all unsuitable to my subject if I mention to you some particulars relative to the leading principles, and capital works of those who excelled in the great style, that I may bring you from abstraction nearer to practice, and by exemplifying the propositions which I have laid down, enable you to understand more clearly what I would enforce.

The principal works of modern art are in fresco, a mode of painting which excludes attention to minute elegancies: yet these works in fresco are the productions on which the fame of the greatest masters depend: such are the pictures of Michael Angelo and Raffaelle in the Vatican, to which we may add the cartoons, which, though not strictly to be called fresco, yet may be put under that denomination; and such are the works of Giulio Romano at Mantua. If these performances were destroyed, with them would be lost the best part of the reputation of those illustrious painters, for these are justly considered as the greatest efforts of our art which the world can boast. To these, therefore, we should principally direct our attention for higher excellences. As for the lower arts, as they have been once discovered, they may be easily attained by those possessed of the former.

Raffaelle, who stands in general foremost of the first painters, owes his reputation, as I have observed, to his excellence in the higher parts of the art. Therefore, his works in fresco ought to be the first object of our study and attention. His easel-works stand in a lower degree of estimation; for though he continually, to the day of his death, embellished his works more and more with the addition of these lower ornaments, which entirely make the merit of some, yet he never arrived at such perfection as to make him an object of imitation. He never was able to conquer perfectly that dryness, or even littleness of manner, which he inherited from his master. He never acquired that nicety of taste in colours, that breadth of light and shadow, that art and management of uniting light, to light, and shadow to shadow, so as to make the object rise out of the ground with that plenitude of effect so much admired in the works of Correggio. When he painted in oil, his hand seemed to be so cramped and confined that he not only lost that facility and spirit, but I think even that correctness of form, which is so perfect and admirable in his fresco works. I do not recollect any pictures of his of this kind, except perhaps the "Transfiguration," in which there are not some parts that appear to be even feebly drawn. That this is not a necessary attendant on oil-painting, we have abundant instances in more modern painters. Lodovico Caracci, for instance, preserved in his works in oil the same spirit, vigour, and correctness, which he had in fresco. I have no desire to degrade Raffaelle from the high rank which he deservedly holds: but by comparing him with himself, he does not appear to me to be the same man in oil as in fresco.

From those who have ambition to tread in this great walk of the art, Michael Angelo claims the next attention. He did not possess so many excellences as Raffaelle, but those he had were of the highest kind. He considered the art as consisting of little more than what may be attained by sculpture, correctness of form, and energy of character. We ought not to expect more than an artist intends in his work. He never attempted those lesser elegancies and graces in the art. Vasari says, he never painted but one picture in oil, and resolved never to paint another, saying it was an employment only fit for women and children.

If any man had a right to look down upon the lower accomplishments as beneath his attention, it was certainly Michael Angelo: nor can it be thought strange that such a mind should have slighted or have been withheld from paying due attention to all those graces and embellishments of art which have diffused such lustre over the works of other painters.

It must be acknowledged likewise, that together with these, which we wish he had more attended to, he has rejected all the false though specious ornaments which disgrace the works even of the most esteemed artists; and I will venture to say, that when those higher excellences are more known and cultivated by the artists and the patrons of arts, his fame and credit will increase with our increasing knowledge. His name will then be held in the same veneration as it was in the enlightened age of Leo the Tenth: and it is remarkable that the reputation of this truly great man has been continually declining as the art itself has declined. For I must remark to you, that it has long been much on the decline, and that our only hope of its revival will consist in your being thoroughly sensible of its depravation and decay. It is to Michael Angelo that we owe even the existence of Raffaelle; it is to him Raffaelle owes the grandeur of his style. He was taught by him to elevate his thoughts, and to conceive his subjects with dignity. His genius, however, formed to blaze and to shine, might, like fire in combustible matter, for ever have lain dormant if it had not caught a spark by its contact with Michael Angelo: and though it never burst out with that extraordinary heat and vehemence, yet it must be acknowledged to be a more pure, regular, and chaste flame. Though our judgment will upon the whole decide in favour of Raffaelle: yet he never takes that firm hold and entire possession of the mind in such a manner as to desire nothing else, and feel nothing wanting. The effect of the capital works of Michael Angelo perfectly correspond to what Bourchardon said he felt from reading Homer. His whole frame appeared to himself to be enlarged, and all nature which surrounded him diminished to atoms.

If we put those great artists in a light of comparison with each other, Raffaelle had more taste and fancy, Michael Angelo more genius and imagination. The one excelled in beauty, the other in energy. Michael Angelo has more of the poetical inspiration; his ideas are vast and sublime; his people are a superior order of beings; there is nothing about them, nothing in the air of their actions or their attitudes, or the style and cast of their very limbs or features, that puts one in mind of their belonging, to our own species. Raffaelle's imagination is not so elevated; his figures are not so much disjoined from our own diminutive race of beings, though his ideas are chaste, noble, and of great conformity to their subjects. Michael Angelo's works have a strong, peculiar, and marked character; they seem to proceed from his own mind entirely, and that mind so rich and abundant, that he never needed, or seemed to disdain, to look abroad for foreign help.

Raffaelle's materials are generally borrowed, though the noble structure is his own. The excellency of this extraordinary man lay in the propriety, beauty, and majesty of his characters, his judicious contrivance of his composition, correctness of drawing, purity of taste, and the skilful accommodation of other men's conceptions to his own purpose. Nobody excelled him in that judgment, with which he united to his own observations on nature the energy of Michael Angelo, and the beauty and simplicity of the antique. To the question, therefore, which ought to hold the first rank, Raffaelle or Michael Angelo, it must be answered, that if it is to be given to him who possessed a greater combination of the higher qualities of the art than any other man, there is no doubt but Raffaelle is the first. But if, according to Longinus, the sublime, being the highest excellence that human composition can attain to, abundantly compensates the absence of every other beauty, and atones for all other deficiencies, then Michael Angelo demands the preference.

These two extraordinary men carried some of the higher excellences of the art to a greater degree of perfection than probably they ever arrived at before. They certainly have not been excelled, nor equalled since. Many of their successors were induced to leave this great road as a beaten path, endeavouring to surprise and please by something uncommon or new. When this desire after novelty has proceeded from mere idleness or caprice, it is not worth the trouble of criticism; but when it has been in consequence of a busy mind of a peculiar complexion, it is always striking and interesting, never insipid.

Such is the great style as it appears in those who possessed it at its height; in this, search after novelty in conception or in treating the subject has no place.

But there is another style, which, though inferior to the former, has still great merit, because it shows that those who cultivated it were men of lively and vigorous imagination. This I call the original or characteristical style; this, being less referred to any true architype existing either in general or particular nature, must be supported by the painter's consistency in the principles he has assumed, and in the union and harmony of his whole design. The excellency of every style, but I think of the subordinate ones more especially, will very much depend on preserving that union and harmony between all the component parts, that they appear to hang well together, as if the whole proceeded from one mind. It is in the works of art, as in the characters of men. The faults or defects of some men seem to become them when they appear to be the natural growth, and of a piece with the rest of their character. A faithful picture of a mind, though it be not of the most elevated kind, though it be irregular, wild, and incorrect, yet if it be marked with that spirit and firmness which characterises works of genius, will claim attention, and be more striking than a combination of excellences that do not seem to hang well together, or we may say than a work that possesses even all excellences, but those in a moderate degree.

One of the strongest marked characters of this kind, which must be allowed to be subordinate to the great style, is that of Salvator Rosa. He gives us a peculiar cast of nature, which, though void of all grace, elegance, and simplicity; though it has nothing of that elevation and dignity which belongs to the grand style, yet has that sort of dignity which belongs to savage and uncultivated nature. But what is most to be admired in him is the perfect correspondence which he observed between the subjects which he chose, and his manner of treating them. Everything is of a piece: his rocks, trees, sky, even to his handling have the same rude and wild character which animates his figures.

To him we may contrast the character of Carlo Maratti, who, in my own opinion, had no great vigour of mind or strength of original genius. He rarely seizes the imagination by exhibiting the higher excellences, nor does he captivate us by that originality which attends the painter who thinks for himself. He knew and practised all the rules of art, and from a composition of Raffaelle, Caracci, and Guido, made up a style, of which its only fault was, that it had no manifest defects and no striking beauties, and that the principles of his composition are never blended together, so as to form one uniform body, original in its kind, or excellent in any view.

I will mention two other painters who, though entirely dissimilar, yet by being each consistent with himself, and possessing a manner entirely his own, have both gained reputation, though for very opposite accomplishments.

The painters I mean are Rubens and Poussin. Rubens I mention in this place, as I think him a remarkable instance of the same mind being seen in all the various parts of the art. The whole is so much of a piece that one can scarce be brought to believe but that if any one of them had been more correct and perfect, his works would not be so complete as they now appear. If we should allow a greater purity and correctness of drawing, his want of simplicity in composition, colouring, and drapery would appear more gross.

In his composition his art is too apparent. His figures have expression, and act with energy, but without simplicity or dignity. His colouring, in which he is eminently skilled, is, notwithstanding, too much of what we call tinted. Throughout the whole of his works there is a proportionable want of that nicety of distinction and elegance of mind which is required in the higher walks of painting; and to this want it may be in some degree ascribed that those qualities which make the excellency of this subordinate style appear in him with their greatest lustre. Indeed, the facility with which he invented, the richness of his composition, the luxuriant harmony and brilliancy of his colouring, so dazzle the eye, that whilst his works continue before us we cannot help thinking that all his deficiencies are fully supplied.

Opposed to this florid, careless, loose, and inaccurate style, that of the simple, careful, pure, and correct style of Poussin seems to be a complete contrast.

Yet however opposite their characters, in one thing they agreed, both of them having a perfect correspondence between all the parts of their respective manners.

One is not sure but every alteration of what is considered as defective in either, would destroy the effect of the whole.

Poussin lived and conversed with the ancient statues so long, that he may be said to be better acquainted with then than with the people who were about him. I have often thought that he carried his veneration for them so far as to wish to give his works the air of ancient paintings. It is certain he copied some of the antique paintings, particularly the "Marriage in the Albrobrandini Palace at Rome," which I believe to be the best relique of those remote ages that has yet been found.

No works of any modern has so much of the air of antique painting as those of Poussin. His best performances have a remarkable dryness of manner, which, though by no means to be recommended for imitation, yet seems perfectly correspondent to that ancient simplicity which distinguishes his style. Like Polidoro he studied them so much, that he acquired a habit of thinking in their way, and seemed to know perfectly the actions and gestures they would use on every occasion.

Poussin in the latter part of his life changed from his dry manner to one much softer and richer, where there is a greater union between the figures and the ground, such as the "Seven Sacraments" in the Duke of Orleans' collection; but neither these, nor any in this manner, are at all comparable to many in his dry manner which we have in England.

The favourite subjects of Poussin were ancient fables; and no painter was ever better qualified to paint such subjects, not only from his being eminently skilled in the knowledge of ceremonies, customs, and habits of the ancients, but from his being so well acquainted with the different characters which those who invented them gave their allegorical figures. Though Rubens has shown great fancy in his Satyrs, Silenuses, and Fauns, yet they are not that distinct separate class of beings which is carefully exhibited by the ancients and by Poussin. Certainly when such subjects of antiquity are represented, nothing in the picture ought to remind us of modern times. The mind is thrown back into antiquity, and nothing ought to be introduced that may tend to awaken it from the illusion.

Poussin seemed to think that the style and the language in which such stories are told is not the worse for preserving some relish of the old way of painting which seemed to give a general uniformity to the whole, so that the mind was thrown back into antiquity not only by the subject, but the execution.

If Poussin, in imitation of the ancients, represents Apollo driving his chariot out of the sea by way of representing the sun rising, if he personifies lakes and rivers, it is no ways offensive in him; but seems perfectly of a piece with the general air of the picture. On the contrary, if the figures which people his pictures had a modern air or countenance, if they appeared like our countrymen, if the draperies were like cloth or silk of our manufacture, if the landscape had the appearance of a modern view, how ridiculous would Apollo appear instead of the sun, an old man or a nymph with an urn instead of a river or lake.

I cannot avoid mentioning here a circumstance in portrait painting which may help to confirm what has been said.

When a portrait is painted in the historical style, as it is neither an exact minute representation of an individual nor completely ideal, every circumstance ought to correspond to this mixture. The simplicity of the antique air and attitude, however much to be admired, is ridiculous when joined to a figure in a modern dress. It is not to my purpose to enter into the question at present, whether this mixed style ought to be adopted or not; yet if it is chosen it is necessary it should be complete and all of a piece: the difference of stuffs, for instance, which make the clothing, should be distinguished in the same degree as the head deviates from a general idea.

Without this union, which I have so often recommended, a work can have no marked and determined character, which is the peculiar and constant evidence of genius. But when this is accomplished to a high degree, it becomes in some sort a rival to that style which we have fixed as the highest.

Thus I have given a sketch of the characters of Rubens and Salvator Rosa, as they appear to me to have the greatest uniformity of mind throughout their whole work. But we may add to these, all these artists who are at the head of the class, and have had a school of imitators from Michael Angelo down to Watteau. Upon the whole it appears that setting aside the ornamental style, there are two different paths, either of which a student may take without degrading the dignity of his art. The first is to combine the higher excellences and embellish them to the greatest advantage. The other is to carry one of these excellences to the highest degree. But those who possess neither must be classed with them, who, as Shakespeare says, are men of no mark or likelihood.

I inculcate as frequently as I can your forming yourselves upon great principles and great models. Your time will be much misspent in every other pursuit. Small excellences should be viewed, not studied; they ought to be viewed, because nothing ought to escape a painter's observation, but for no other reason.

There is another caution which I wish to give you. Be as select in those whom you endeavour to please, as in those whom you endeavour to imitate. Without the love of fame you can never do anything excellent; but by an excessive and undistinguishing thirst after it, you will come to have vulgar views; you will degrade your style; and your taste will be entirely corrupted. It is certain that the lowest style will be the most popular, as it falls within the compass of ignorance itself; and the vulgar will always be pleased with what is natural in the confined and misunderstood sense of the word.

One would wish that such depravation of taste should be counteracted, with such manly pride as Euripides expressed to the Athenians, who criticised his works, "I do not compose," says he, "my works in order to be corrected by you, but to instruct you." It is true, to have a right to speak thus, a man must be a Euripides. However, thus much may be allowed, that when an artist is sure that he is upon firm ground, supported by the authority and practice of his predecessors of the greatest reputation, he may then assume the boldness and intrepidity of genius; at any rate, he must not be tempted out of the right path by any tide of popularity that always accompanies the lower styles of painting.

I mention this, because our exhibitions, that produce such admirable effects by nourishing emulation, and calling out genius, have also a mischievous tendency by seducing the painter to an ambition of pleasing indiscriminately the mixed multitude of people who resort to them.

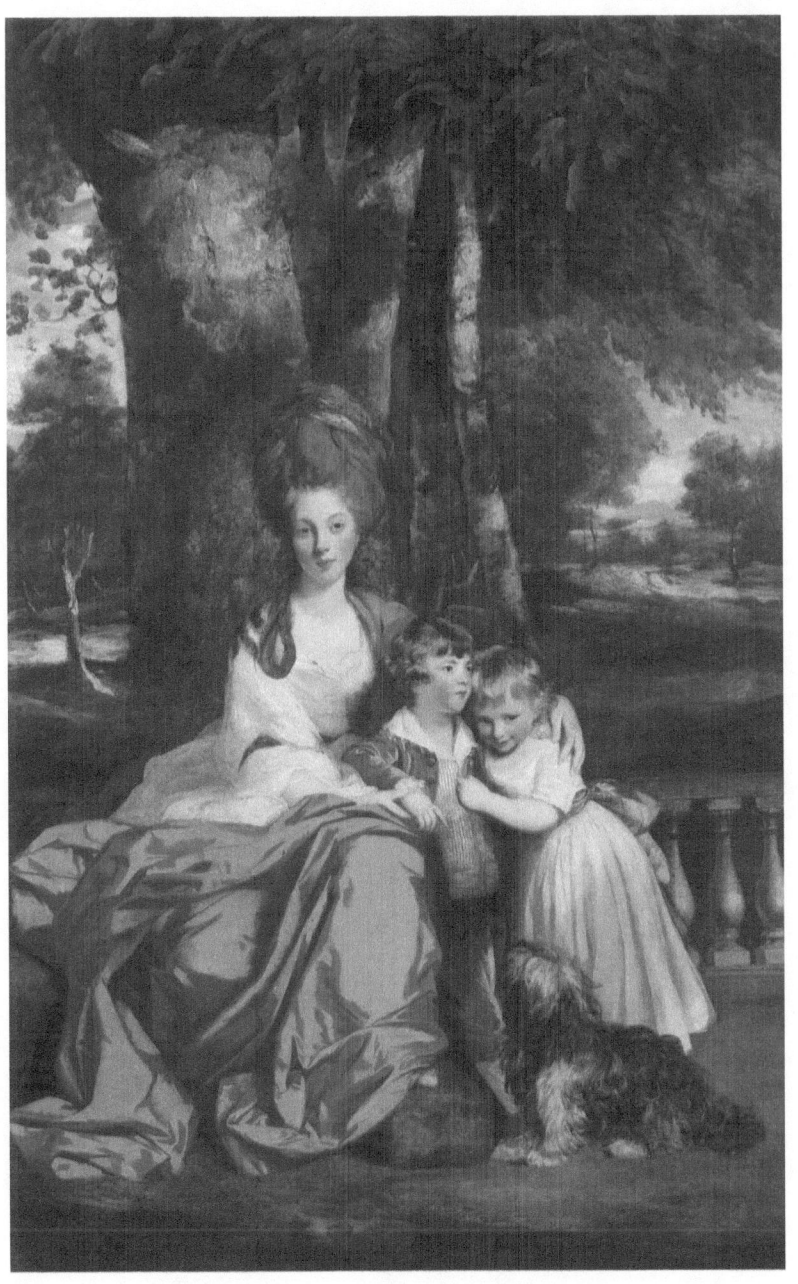

Joshua Reynolds
Lady Elizabeth Delmé and Her Children
1777-1779
oil on canvas, 238 x 147 cm
Andrew W. Mellon Collection
National Gallery of Art, Washington

DISCOURSE VI

**Delivered to the Students of the Royal Academy
on the Distribution of the Prizes
December 10, 1774
by the President**

Gentlemen, — When I have taken the liberty of addressing you on the course and order of your studies, I never proposed to enter into a minute detail of the art. This I have always left to the several professors, who pursue the end of our institution with the highest honour to themselves, and with the greatest advantage to the students.

My purpose in the discourses I have held in the Academy is to lay down certain general ideas, which seem to me proper for the formation of a sound taste; principles necessary to guard the pupils against those errors into which the sanguine temper common at their time of life, has a tendency to lead them, and which have rendered abortive the hopes of so many successions of promising young men in all parts of Europe.

I wish, also, to intercept and suppress those prejudices which particularly prevail when the mechanism of painting is come to its perfection, and which when they do prevail are certain to prevail to the utter destruction of the higher and more valuable parts of this literate and liberal profession.

These two have been my principal purposes; they are still as much my concern as ever; and if I repeat my own ideas on the subject, you who know how fast mistake and prejudice, when neglected, gain ground upon truth and reason, will easily excuse me. I only attempt to set the same thing in the greatest variety of lights.

The subject of this discourse will be imitation, as far as a painter is concerned in it. By imitation I do not mean imitation in its largest sense, but simply the following of other masters, and the advantage to be drawn from the study of their works.

Those who have undertaken to write on our art, and have represented it as a kind of inspiration, as a gift bestowed upon peculiar favourites at their birth, seem to ensure a much more favourable disposition from their readers, and have a much more captivating and liberal air, than he who goes about to examine, coldly, whether there are any means by which this art may be acquired; how our mind may be strengthened and expanded, and what guides will show the way to eminence.

It is very natural for those who are unacquainted with the cause of anything extraordinary to be astonished at the effect, and to consider it as a kind of magic. They, who have never observed the gradation by which art is acquired, who see only what is the full result of long labour and application of an infinite number, and infinite variety of acts, are apt to conclude from their entire inability to do the same at once, that it is not only inaccessible to themselves, but can be done by those only who have some gift of the nature of inspiration bestowed upon them.

The travellers into the East tell us that when the ignorant inhabitants of these countries are asked concerning the ruins of stately edifices yet remaining amongst them, the melancholy monuments of their former grandeur and long-lost science, they always answer that they were built by magicians. The untaught mind finds a vast gulf between its own powers and these works of complicated art which it is utterly unable to fathom. And it supposes that such a void can be passed only by supernatural powers.

And, as for artists themselves, it is by no means their interest to undeceive such judges, however conscious they may be of the very natural means by which the extraordinary powers were acquired; our art being intrinsically imitative, rejects this idea of inspiration more, perhaps, than any other.

It is to avoid this plain confession of truth, as it should seem, that this imitation of masters—indeed, almost all imitation which implies a more regular and progressive method of attaining the ends of painting—has ever been particularly inveighed against with great keenness, both by ancient and modern writers.

To derive all from native power, to owe nothing to another, is the praise which men, who do not much think what they are saying, bestow sometimes upon others, and sometimes on themselves; and their imaginary dignity is naturally heightened by a supercilious censure of the low, the barren, the grovelling, the servile imitator. It would be no wonder if a student, frightened by these terrors and disgraceful epithets, with which the poor imitators are so often loaded, should let fall his pencil in mere despair, conscious how much he has been indebted to the labours of others, how little, how very little of his art was born with him; and, considering it as hopeless, to set about acquiring by the imitation of any human master what he is taught to suppose is matter of inspiration from heaven.

Some allowance must be made for what is said in the gaiety or ambition of rhetoric. We cannot suppose that any one can really mean to exclude all imitation of others. A position so wild would scarce deserve a serious answer, for it is apparent, if we were forbid to make use of the advantages which our predecessors afford us, the art would be always to begin, and consequently remain always in its infant state; and it is a common observation that no art was ever invented and carried to perfection at the same time.

But to bring us entirely to reason and sobriety, let it be observed, that a painter must not only be of necessity an imitator of the works of nature, which alone is sufficient to dispel this phantom of inspiration, but he must be as necessarily an imitator of the works of other painters. This appears more humiliating, but it is equally true; and no man can be an artist, whatever he may suppose, upon any other terms.

However, those who appear more moderate and reasonable allow that study is to begin by imitation, but that we should no longer use the thoughts of our predecessors when we are become able to think for ourselves. They hold that imitation is as hurtful to the more advanced student as it was advantageous to the beginner.

For my own part, I confess I am not only very much disposed to lay down the absolute necessity of imitation in the first stages of the art, but am of opinion that the study of other masters, which I here call imitation, may be extended throughout our whole life without any danger of the inconveniences with which it is charged, of enfeebling the mind, or preventing us from giving that original air which every work undoubtedly ought always to have.

I am, on the contrary, persuaded that by imitation only, variety, and even originality of invention is produced.

I will go further; even genius, at least what generally is so called, is the child of imitation. But as this appears to be contrary to the general opinion, I must explain my position before I enforce it.

Genius is supposed to be a power of producing excellences which are out of the reach of the rules of art—a power which no precepts can teach, and which no industry can acquire.

This opinion of the impossibility of acquiring those beauties which stamp the work with the character of genius, supposes that it is something more fixed than in reality it is, and that we always do, and ever did agree, about what should be considered as a characteristic of genius.

But the truth is that the degree of excellence which proclaims genius is different in different times and different places; and what shows it to be so is that mankind have often changed their opinion upon this matter.

When the arts were in their infancy, the power of merely drawing the likeness of any object was considered as one of its greatest efforts.

The common people, ignorant of the principles of art, talk the same language even to this day. But when it was found that every man could be taught to do this, and a great deal more, merely by the observance of certain precepts, the name of genius then shifted its application, and was given only to those who added the peculiar character of the object they represented; to those who had invention, expression, grace, or dignity; or, in short, such qualities or excellences the producing of which could not then be taught by any known and promulgated rules.

We are very sure that the beauty of form, the expression of the passions, the art of composition, even the power of giving a general air of grandeur to your work, is at present very much under the dominion of rules. These excellences were, heretofore, considered merely as the effects of genius; and justly, if genius is not taken for inspiration, but as the effect of close observation and experience.

He who first made any of these observations and digested them, so as to form an invariable principle for himself to work by, had that merit; but probably no one went very far at once; and generally the first who gave the hint did not know how to pursue it steadily and methodically, at least not in the beginning. He himself worked on it, and improved it; others worked more, and improved farther, until the secret was discovered, and the practice made as general as refined practice can be made. How many more principles may be fixed and ascertained we cannot tell; but as criticism is likely to go hand in hand with the art which is its subject, we may venture to say that as that art shall advance, its powers will be still more and more fixed by rules.

But by whatever strides criticism may gain ground, we need be under no apprehension that invention will ever be annihilated or subdued, or intellectual energy be brought entirely within the restraint of written law. Genius will still have room enough to expatiate, and keep always the same distance from narrow comprehension and mechanical performance.

What we now call genius begins, not where rules, abstractedly taken, end, but where known vulgar and trite rules have no longer any place. It must of necessity be that even works of genius, as well as every other effect, as it must have its cause, must likewise have its rules; it cannot be by chance that excellences are produced with any constancy, or any certainty, for this is not the nature of chance, but the rules by which men of extraordinary parts, and such as are called men of genius work, are either such as they discover by their own peculiar observation, or of such a nice texture as not easily to admit handling or expressing in words, especially as artists are not very frequently skilful in that mode of communicating ideas.

Unsubstantial, however, as these rules may seem, and difficult as it may be to convey them in writing, they are still seen and felt in the mind of the artist, and he works from them with as much certainty as if they were embodied, as I may say, upon paper. It is true these refined principles cannot be always made palpable, like the more gross rules of art; yet it does not follow but that the mind may be put in such a train that it shall perceive, by a kind of scientific sense, that propriety which words, particularly words of unpracticed writers such as we are, can but very feebly suggest.

Invention is one of the great marks of genius, but if we consult experience, we shall find that it is by being conversant with the inventions of others that we learn to invent, as by reading the thoughts of others we learn to think.

Whoever has so far formed his taste as to be able to relish and feel the beauties of the great masters has gone a great way in his study; for, merely from a consciousness of this relish of the right, the mind swells with an inward pride, and is almost as powerfully affected as if it had itself produced what it admires. Our hearts frequently warmed in this manner by the contact of those whom we wish to resemble, will undoubtedly catch something of their way of thinking, and we shall receive in our own bosoms some radiation at least of their fire and splendour. That disposition, which is so strong in children, still continues with us, of catching involuntarily the general air and manner of those with whom we are most conversant; with this difference only, that a young mind is naturally pliable and imitative, but in a more advanced state it grows rigid, and must be warmed and softened before it will receive a deep impression.

From these considerations, which a little of your reflection will carry a great way further, it appears of what great consequence it is that our minds should be habituated to the contemplation of excellence, and that, far from being contented to make such habits the discipline of our youth only, we should, to the last moment of our lives, continue a settled intercourse with all the true examples of grandeur. Their inventions are not only the food of our infancy, but the substance which supplies the fullest maturity of our vigour.

The mind is but a barren soil; is a soil soon exhausted, and will produce no crop, or only one, unless it be continually fertilised and enriched with foreign matter.

When we have had continually before us the great works of art to impregnate our minds with kindred ideas, we are then, and not till then, fit to produce something, of the same species. We behold all about us with the eyes of these penetrating observers, and our minds, accustomed to think the thoughts of the noblest and brightest intellects, are prepared for the discovery and selection of all that is great and noble in nature. The greatest natural genius cannot subsist on its own stock: he who resolves never to ransack any mind but his own will be soon reduced, from mere barrenness, to the poorest of all imitations; he will be obliged to imitate himself, and to repeat what he has before often repeated. When we know the subject designed by such men, it will never be difficult to guess what kind of work is to be produced.

It is vain for painters or poets to endeavour to invent without materials on which the mind may work, and from which invention must originate. Nothing can come of nothing.

Homer is supposed to be possessed of all the learning of his time. And we are certain that Michael Angelo and Raffaelle were equally possessed of all knowledge in the art which was discoverable in the works of their predecessors.

A mind enriched by an assemblage of all the treasures of ancient

and modern art will be more elevated and fruitful in resources in proportion to the number of ideas which have been carefully collected
and thoroughly digested. There can be no doubt that he who has the
most materials has the greatest means of invention; and if he has not
the power of using them, it must proceed from a feebleness of intellect
or from the confused manner in which those collections have been
laid up in his mind.

The addition of other men's judgment is so far from weakening,
as is the opinion of many, our own, that it will fashion and consolidate
those ideas of excellence which lay in their birth feeble, ill-shaped,
and confused, but which are finished and put in order by the authority
and practice of those whose works may be said to have been conse-
crated by having stood the test of ages.

The mind, or genius, has been compared to a spark of fire which is
smothered by a heap of fuel and prevented from blazing into a flame.
This simile, which is made use of by the younger Pliny, may be easily
mistaken for argument or proof.

There is no danger of the mind's being over-burdened with knowledge, or the genius extinguished by any addition of images; on the
contrary, these acquisitions may as well, perhaps better, be compared,
if comparisons signified anything in reasoning, to the supply of living
embers, which will contribute to strengthen the spark that without the
association of more would have died away.

The truth is, he whose feebleness is such as to make other men's
thoughts an incumbrance to him can have no very great strength of
mind or genius of his own to be destroyed, so that not much harm will
be done at worst.

We may oppose to Pliny the greater authority of Cicero, who is
continually enforcing the necessity of this method of study. In his dia-
logue on Oratory he makes Crassus say, that one of the first and most
important precepts is to choose a proper model for our imitation. *Hoc
fit primum in preceptis meis ut demonstremus quem imitemur.*

When I speak of the habitual imitation and continued study of
masters, it is not to be understood that I advise any endeavour to copy
the exact peculiar colour and complexion of another man's mind; the
success of such an attempt must always be like his who imitates exactly
the air, manner, and gestures of him whom he admires. His model
may be excellent, but the copy will be ridiculous; this ridicule does

not arise from his having imitated, but from his not having chosen the right mode of imitation.

It is a necessary and warrantable pride to disdain to walk servilely behind any individual, however elevated his rank. The true and liberal ground of imitation is an open field, where, though he who precedes has had the advantage of starting before you, yet it is enough to pursue his course; you need not tread in his footsteps, and you certainly have a right to outstrip him if you can.

Nor, whilst I recommend studying the art from artists, can I be supposed to mean that nature is to be neglected? I take this study in aid and not in exclusion of the other. Nature is, and must be, the fountain which alone is inexhaustible; and from which all excellences must originally flow.

The great use of studying our predecessors is to open the mind, to shorten our labour, and to give us the result of the selection made by those great minds of what is grand or beautiful in nature: her rich stores are all spread out before us; but it is an art, and no easy art, to know how or what to choose, and how to attain and secure the object of our choice.

Thus the highest beauty of form must be taken from nature; but it is an art of long deduction and great experience to know how to find it.

We must not content ourselves with merely admiring and relishing; we must enter into the principles on which the work is wrought; these do not swim on the superficies, and consequently are not open to superficial observers.

Art in its perfection is not ostentatious; it lies hid, and works its effect itself unseen. It is the proper study and labour of an artist to uncover and find out the latent cause of conspicuous beauties, and from thence form principles for his own conduct; such an examination is a continual exertion of the mind, as great, perhaps, as that of the artist whose works he is thus studying.

The sagacious imitator not only remarks what distinguishes the different manner or genius of each master; he enters into the contrivance in the composition, how the masses of lights are disposed, the means by which the effect is produced, how artfully some parts are lost in the ground, others boldly relieved, and how all these are mutually altered and interchanged according to the reason and scheme of the work. He admires not the harmony of colouring alone, but he examines by what artifice one colour is a foil to its neighbour. He looks close into the tints, of what colours they are composed, till he has formed clear and distinct ideas, and has learnt to see in what harmony and good colouring consists. What is learnt in this manner from the works of others becomes really our own, sinks deep, and is never forgotten; nay, it is by seizing on this clue that we proceed forward, and get further and further in enlarging the principle and improving the practice.

There can be no doubt but the art is better learnt from the works themselves than from the precepts which are formed upon these works; but if it is difficult to choose proper models for imitation, it requires no less circumspection to separate and distinguish what in those models we ought to imitate.

I cannot avoid mentioning here, though it is not my intention at present to enter into the art and method of study, an error which students are too apt to fall into.

He that is forming himself must look with great caution and wariness on those peculiarities, or prominent parts, which at first force themselves upon view, and are the marks, or what is commonly called the manner, by which that individual artist is distinguished.

Peculiar marks I hold to be generally, if not always, defects, however difficult it may be, wholly to escape them.

Peculiarities in the works of art are like those in the human figure; it is by them that we are cognisable and distinguished one from another, but they are always so many blemishes, which, however, both in the one case and in the other, cease to appear deformities to those who have them continually before their eyes. In the works of art, even the most enlightened mind, when warmed by beauties of the highest kind, will by degrees find a repugnance within him to acknowledge any defects; nay, his enthusiasm will carry him so far as to transform them into beauties and objects of imitation.

It must be acknowledged that a peculiarity of style, either from its novelty, or by seeming to proceed from a peculiar turn of mind, often escapes blame; on the contrary, it is sometimes striking and pleasing; but this it is vain labour to endeavour to imitate, because novelty and peculiarity being its only merit, when it ceases to be new, it ceases to have value.

A manner, therefore, being a defect, and every painter, however excellent, having a manner, it seems to follow that all kinds of faults, as well as beauties, may be learned under the sanction of the greatest authorities.

Even the great name of Michael Angelo may be used to keep in countenance a deficiency, or rather neglect of colouring, and every other ornamental part of the art.

If the young student is dry and hard, Poussin is the same. If his work has a careless and unfinished air, he has most of the Venetian School to support him. If he makes no selection of objects, but takes individual nature just as he finds it, he is like Rembrandt. If he is incorrect in the proportions of his figures, Correggio was likewise incorrect. If his colours are not blended and united, Rubens was equally crude.

In short, there is no defect but may be excused, if it is a sufficient excuse that it can be imputed to considerable artists; but it must be remembered that it was not by these defects they acquired their reputation: they have a right to our pardon, but not to our admiration.

However, to imitate peculiarities or mistake defects for beauties that man will be most liable who confines his imitation to one favourite master; and, even though he chooses the best, and is capable of distinguishing the real excellences of his model, it is not by such narrow practice that a genius or mastery in the art is acquired. A man is as little likely to form a true idea of the perfection of the art by studying a single artist as he would be of producing a perfectly beautiful figure by an exact imitation of any individual living model.

And as the painter, by bringing together in one piece those beauties which are dispersed amongst a great variety of individuals, produces a figure more beautiful than can be found in nature, so that artist who can unite in himself the excellences of the various painters, will approach nearer to perfection than any one of his masters.

He who confines himself to the imitation of an individual, as he never proposes to surpass, so he is not likely to equal, the object of imitation. He professes only to follow, and he that follows must necessarily be behind.

We should imitate the conduct of the great artists in the course of their studies, as well as the works which they produced, when they were perfectly formed. Raffaelle began by imitating implicitly the manner of Pietro Perugino, under whom he studied; so his first works are scarce to be distinguished from his master's; but soon forming higher and more extensive views, he imitated the grand outline of Michael Angelo. He learnt the manner of using colours from the works of Leonardo da Vinci and Fratre Bartolomeo: to all this he added the contemplation of all the remains of antiquity that were within his reach, and employed others to draw for him what was in Greece and distant places. And it is from his having taken so many models that he became himself a model for all succeeding painters, always imitating, and always original.

If your ambition therefore be to equal Raffaelle, you must do as Raffaelle did; take many models, and not take even him for your guide alone to the exclusion of others. And yet the number is infinite of those who seem, if one may judge by their style, to have seen no other works but those of their master, or of some favourite whose manner is their first wish and their last.

I will mention a few that occur to me of this narrow, confined, illiberal, unscientific, and servile kind of imitators. Guido was thus meanly copied by Elizabetta Sirani, and Simone Cantarini; Poussin, by Verdier and Cheron; Parmigiano, by Jeronimo Mazzuoli; Paolo Veronese and Iacomo Bassan had for their imitators their brothers and sons; Pietro de Cortona was followed by Ciro Ferri and Romanelli; Rubens, by Jacques Jordans and Diepenbeck; Guercino, by his own family, the Gennari; Carlo Marratti was imitated by Giuseppe Chiari and Pietro da Pietri; and Rembrandt, by Bramer, Eckhout, and Flink. All these, to whom may be added a much longer list of painters, whose works among the ignorant pass for those of their masters, are justly to be censured for barrenness and servility.

To oppose to this list a few that have adopted a more liberal style of imitation: Pelegrino Tibaldi, Rosso, and Primaticio did not coldly imitate, but caught something of the fire that animates the works of Michael Angelo. The Carraches formed their style from Pelegrino Tibaldi, Correggio, and the Venetian School. Domenichino, Guido, Lanfranco, Albano, Guercino, Cavidone, Schidone, Tiarini, though it is sufficiently apparent that they came from the School of the Carraches, have yet the appearance of men who extended their views beyond the model that lay before them, and have shown that they had opinions of their own, and thought for themselves, after they had made themselves masters of the general principles of their schools.

Le Seure's first manner resembles very much that of his master Vovet: but as he soon excelled him, so he differed from him in every part of the art. Carlo Marratti succeeded better than those I have first named, and I think owes his superiority to the extension of his views; besides his master Andrea Sacchi, he imitated Raffaelle, Guido, and the Carraches. It is true, there is nothing very captivating in Carlo Marratti; but this proceeded from wants which cannot be completely supplied; that is, want of strength of parts. In this, certainly men are not equal, and a man can bring home wares only in proportion to the capital with which he goes to market. Carlo, by diligence, made the most of what he had; but there was undoubtedly a heaviness about him, which extended itself, uniformly to his invention, expression, his drawing, colouring, and the general effect of his pictures. The truth is, he never equalled any of his patterns in any one thing, and he added little of his own.

But we must not rest contented, even in this general study of the moderns; we must trace back the art to its fountain head, to that source from whence they drew their principal excellences, the monuments of pure antiquity.

All the inventions and thoughts of the ancients, whether conveyed to us in statues, bas-reliefs, intaglios, cameos, or coins, are to be sought after and carefully studied: The genius that hovers over these venerable relics may be called the father of modern art.

From the remains of the works of the ancients the modern arts were revived, and it is by their means that they must be restored a second time. However it may mortify our vanity, we must be forced to allow them our masters; and we may venture to prophecy, that when they shall cease to be studied, arts will no longer flourish, and we shall again relapse into barbarism.

The fire of the artist's own genius operating upon these materials which have been thus diligently collected, will enable him to make new combinations, perhaps, superior to what had ever before been in the possession of the art. As in the mixture of the variety of metals, which are said to have been melted and run together at the burning of Corinth, a new and till then unknown metal was produced equal in value to any of those that had contributed to its composition. And though a curious refiner may come with his crucibles, analyze and separate its various component parts, yet Corinthian brass would still hold its rank amongst the most beautiful and valuable of metals.

We have hitherto considered the advantages of imitation as it tends to form the taste, and as a practice by which a spark of that genius may be caught which illumines these noble works, that ought always to be present to our thoughts.

We come now to speak of another kind of imitation; the borrowing a particular thought, an action, attitude, or figure, and transplanting it into your own work: this will either come under the charge of plagiarism, or be warrantable, and deserve commendation, according to the address with which it is performed. There is some difference likewise whether it is upon the ancients or the moderns that these depredations are made. It is generally allowed that no man need be ashamed of copying the ancients: their works are considered as a magazine of common property, always open to the public, whence every man has a right to what materials he pleases; and if he has the art of using them, they are supposed to become to all intents and purposes his own property.

The collection which Raffaelle made of the thoughts of the ancients with so much trouble, is a proof of his opinion on this subject. Such collections may be made with much more ease, by means of an art scarce known in his time; I mean that of engraving, by which, at an easy rate, every man may now avail himself of the inventions of antiquity.

It must be acknowledged that the works of the moderns are more the property of their authors; he who borrows an idea from an artist, or perhaps from a modern, not his contemporary, and so accommodates it to his own work that it makes a part of it, with no seam or joining appearing, can hardly be charged with plagiarism; poets practise this kind of borrowing without reserve. But an artist should not be contented with this only; he should enter into a competition with his original, and endeavour to improve what he is appropriating to his own work. Such imitation is so far from having anything in it of the servility of plagiarism, that it is a perpetual exercise of the mind, a continual invention.

Borrowing or stealing with such art and caution will have a right to the same lenity as was used by the Lacedemonians; who did not punish theft, but the want of artifice to conceal it.

In order to encourage you to imitation, to the utmost extent, let me add, that very finished artists in the inferior branches of the art will contribute to furnish the mind and give hints of which a skilful painter, who is sensible of what he wants, and is in no danger of being infected by the contact of vicious models, will know how to avail himself. He will pick up from dunghills what by a nice chemistry, passing through his own mind, shall be converted into pure gold; and, under the rudeness of Gothic essays, he will find original, rational, and even sublime inventions.

In the luxuriant style of Paul Veronese, in the capricious compositions of Tintoret, he will find something that will assist his invention, and give points, from which his own imagination shall rise and take flight, when the subject which he treats will, with propriety, admit of splendid effects.

In every school, whether Venetian, French, or Dutch, he will find either ingenious compositions, extraordinary effects, some peculiar expressions, or some mechanical excellence, well worthy his attention and, in some measure, of his imitation; even in the lower class of the French painters, great beauties are often found united with great defects.

Though Coypel wanted a simplicity of taste, and mistook a presumptuous and assuming air for what is grand and majestic; yet he frequently has good sense and judgment in his manner of telling his stories, great skill in his compositions, and is not without a considerable power of expressing the passions, The modern affectation of grace in his works, as well as in those of Bouche and Watteau, may be said to be separated by a very thin partition from the more simple and pure grace of Correggio and Parmigiano.

Amongst the Dutch painters, the correct, firm, and determined pencil, which was employed by Bamboccio and Jan Miel on vulgar and mean subjects, might without any change be employed on the highest, to which, indeed, it seems more properly to belong. The greatest style, if that style is confined to small figures such as Poussin generally painted, would receive an additional grace by the elegance and precision of pencil so admirable in the works of Teniers.

Though this school more particularly excelled in the mechanism of painting, yet there are many who have shown great abilities in expressing what must be ranked above mechanical excellences.

In the works of Frank Hals the portrait painter may observe the composition of a face, the features well put together as the painters express it, from whence proceeds that strong marked character of individual nature which is so remarkable in his portraits, and is not to be found in an equal degree in any other painter. If he had joined to this most difficult part of the art a patience in finishing what he had so correctly planned, he might justly have claimed the place which Vandyke, all things considered, so justly holds as the first of portrait painters.

Others of the same school have shown great power in expressing the character and passions of those vulgar people which are the subjects of their study and attention. Amongst those, Jean Stein seems to be one of the most diligent and accurate observers of what passed in those scenes which he frequented, and which were to him an academy. I can easily imagine that if this extraordinary man had had the good fortune to have been born in Italy instead of Holland, had he lived in Rome instead of Leyden, and had been blessed with Michael Angelo and Raffaelle for his masters instead of Brower and Van Gowen, that the same sagacity and penetration which distinguished so accurately the different characters and expression in his vulgar figures, would, when exerted in the selection and imitation of what was great and elevated in nature, have been equally successful, and his name would have been now ranged with the great pillars and supporters of our art.

Men who, although thus bound down by the almost invincible powers of early habits, have still exerted extraordinary abilities within their narrow and confined circle, and have, from the natural vigour of their mind, given such an interesting expression, such force and energy to their works, though they cannot be recommended to be exactly imitated, may yet invite an artist to endeavour to transfer, by a kind of parody, those excellences to his own works. Whoever has acquired the power of making this use of the Flemish, Venetian, and French schools is a real genius, and has sources of knowledge open to him which were wanting to the great artists who lived in the great age of painting.

To find excellences however dispersed, to discover beauties however concealed by the multitude of defects with which they are surrounded, can be the work only of him who, having a mind always alive to his art, has extended his views to all ages and to all schools, and has acquired from that comprehensive mass which he has thus gathered to himself, a well digested and perfect idea of his art, to which everything is referred. Like a sovereign judge and arbiter of art, he is possessed of that presiding power which separates and attracts every excellence from every school, selects both from what is great and what is little, brings home knowledge from the east and from the west, making the universe tributary towards furnishing his mind and enriching his works with originality and variety of inventions.

Thus I have ventured to give my opinion of what appears to me the true and only method by which an artist makes himself master of his profession, which I hold ought to be one continued course of imitation, that is not to cease but with our lives.

Those who, either from their own engagements and hurry of business, or from indolence, or from conceit and vanity, have neglected looking out of themselves, as far as my experience and observation reaches, have from that time not only ceased to advance and improve in their performance, but have gone backward. They may be compared to men who have lived upon their principal till they are reduced to beggary and left without resources.

I can recommend nothing better, therefore, than that you endeavour to infuse into your works what you learn from the contemplation of the works of others. To recommend this has the appearance of needless and superfluous advice, but it has fallen within my own knowledge that artists, though they are not wanting in a sincere love for their art, though they have great pleasure in seeing good pictures, and are well skilled to distinguish what is excellent or defective in them, yet go on in their own manner, without any endeavour to give a little of those beauties which they admire in others, to their own works. It is difficult to conceive how the present Italian painters, who live in the midst of the treasures of art, should be contented with their own style. They proceed in their common-place inventions, and never think it worth while to visit the works of those great artists with which they are surrounded.

SIXTH DISCOURSE

I remember several years ago to have conversed at Rome with an artist of great fame throughout Europe; he was not without a considerable degree of abilities, but those abilities were by no means equal to his own opinion of them. From the reputation he had acquired he too fondly concluded that he stood in the same rank, when compared to his predecessors, as he held with regard to his miserable contemporary rivals.

In conversation about some particulars of the works of Raffaelle, he seemed to have, or to affect to have, a very obscure memory of them. He told me that he had not set his foot in the Vatican for fifteen years together; that indeed he had been in treaty to copy a capital picture of Raffaelle, but that the business had gone off; however, if the agreement had held, his copy would have greatly exceeded the original. The merit of this artist, however great we may suppose it, I am sure would have been far greater, and his presumption would have been far less if he had visited the Vatican, as in reason he ought to have done, once at least every month of his life.

I address myself, gentlemen, to you who have made some progress in the art, and are to be for the future under the guidance of your own judgment and discretion.

I consider you as arrived to that period when you have a right to think for yourselves, and to presume that every man is fallible; to study the masters with a suspicion that great men are not always exempt from great faults; to criticise, compare, and rank their works in your own estimation, as they approach to or recede from that standard of perfection which you have formed in your own mind, but which those masters themselves, it must be remembered, have taught you to make, and which you will cease to make with correctness when you cease to study them. It is their excellences which have taught you their defects.

I would wish you to forget where you are, and who it is that speaks to you. I only direct you to higher models and better advisers. We can teach you here but very little; you are henceforth to be your own teachers. Do this justice, however, to the English Academy, to bear in mind, that in this place you contracted no narrow habits, no false ideas, nothing that could lead you to the imitation of any living master, who may be the fashionable darling of the day. As you have not been taught to flatter us, do not learn to flatter yourselves. We have endeavoured to lead you to the admiration of nothing but what is truly admirable. If you choose inferior patterns, or if you make your own *former* works, your patterns for your *latter*, it is your own fault.

The purpose of this discourse, and, indeed, of most of my others, is to caution you against that false opinion, but too prevalent amongst artists, of the imaginary power of native genius, and its sufficiency in great works. This opinion, according to the temper of mind it meets with, almost always produces, either a vain confidence, or a sluggish despair, both equally fatal to all proficiency.

Study, therefore, the great works of the great masters for ever. Study as nearly as you can, in the order, in the manner, on the principles, on which they studied. Study nature attentively, but always with those masters in your company; consider them as models which you are to imitate, and at the same time as rivals which you are to combat.

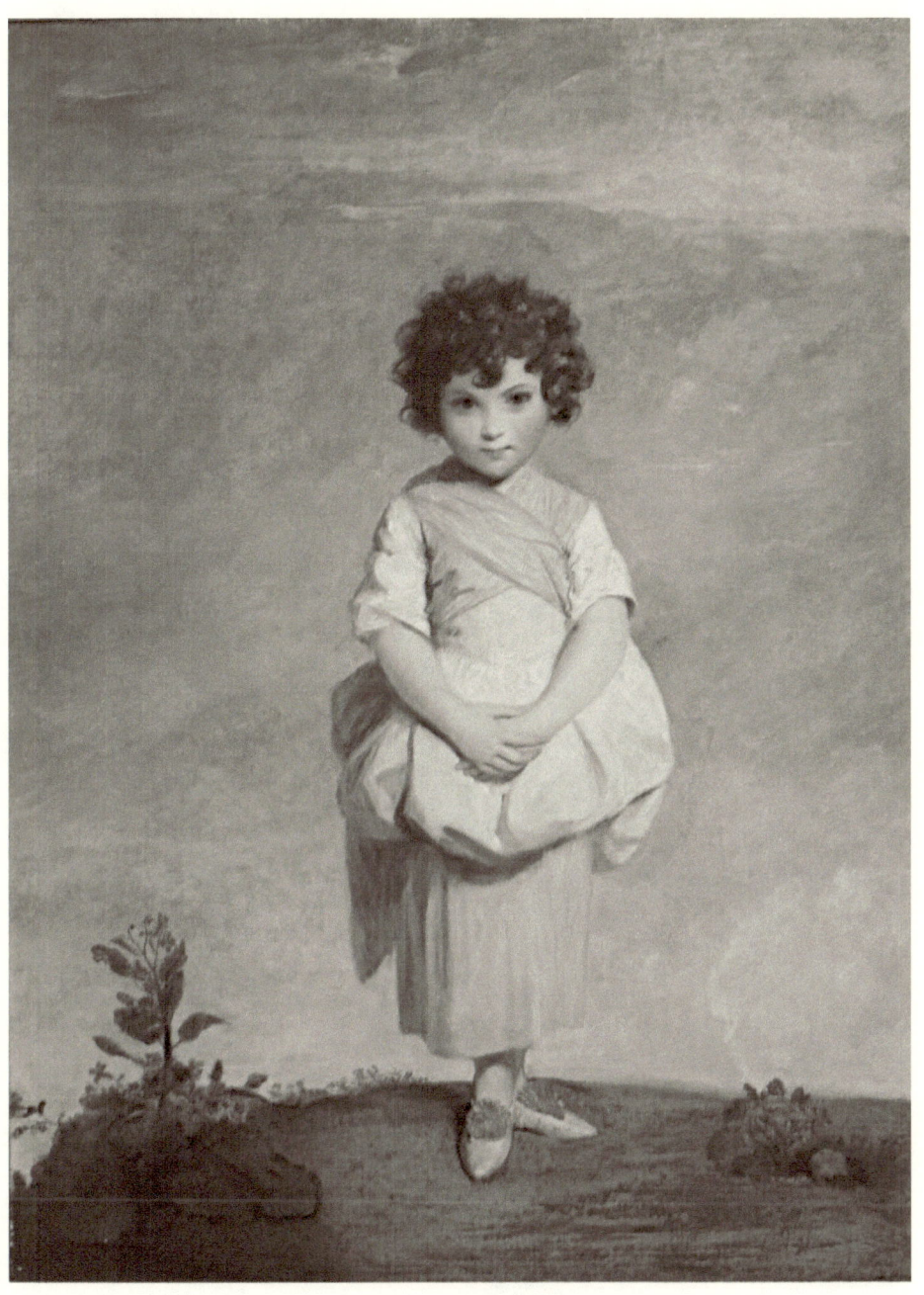

Joshua Reynolds
Collina (Lady Gertrude Fitzpatrick)
1779
oil on canvas
Columbus Museum of Art

DISCOURSE VII

**Delivered to the Students of the Royal Academy
on the Distribution of the Prizes
December 10th, 1776
by the President.**

Gentlemen, — It has been my uniform endeavour, since I first addressed you from this place, to impress you strongly with one ruling idea. I wished you to be persuaded, that success in your art depends almost entirely on your own industry; but the industry which I principally recommended, is not the industry of the *hands*, but of the *mind*.

As our art is not a divine gift, so neither is it a mechanical trade. Its foundations are laid in solid science. And practice, though essential to perfection, can never attain that to which it aims, unless it works under the direction of principle.

Some writers upon art carry this point too far, and suppose that such a body of universal and profound learning is requisite, that the very enumeration of its kind is enough to frighten a beginner. Vitruvius, after going through the many accomplishments of nature, and the many acquirements of learning, necessary to an architect, proceeds with great gravity to assert that he ought to be well skilled in the civil law, that he may not be cheated in the title of the ground he builds on.

But without such exaggeration, we may go so far as to assert, that a painter stands in need of more knowledge than is to be picked off his pallet, or collected by looking on his model, whether it be in life or in picture. He can never be a great artist who is grossly illiterate.

Every man whose business is description ought to be tolerably conversant with the poets in some language or other, that he may imbibe a poetical spirit and enlarge his stock of ideas. He ought to acquire a habit of comparing and divesting his notions. He ought not to be wholly unacquainted with that part of philosophy which gives him an insight into human nature, and relates to the manners, characters, passions, and affections. He ought to know something concerning the mind, as well as a great deal concerning the body of man.

For this purpose, it is not necessary that he should go into such a compass of reading, as must, by distracting his attention, disqualify him for the practical part of his profession, and make him sink the performer in the critic. Reading, if it can be made the favourite recreation of his leisure hours, will improve and enlarge his mind without retarding his actual industry.

What such partial and desultory reading cannot afford, may be supplied by the conversation of learned and ingenious men, which is the best of all substitutes for those who have not the means or opportunities of deep study. There are many such men in this age; and they will be pleased with communicating their ideas to artists, when they see them curious and docile, if they are treated with that respect and deference which is so justly their due. Into such society, young artists, if they make it the point of their ambition, will by degrees be admitted. There, without formal teaching, they will insensibly come to feel and reason like those they live with, and find a rational and systematic taste imperceptibly formed in their minds, which they will know how to reduce to a standard, by applying general truth to their own purposes, better perhaps than those to whom they owed the original sentiment.

Of these studies and this conversation, the desired and legitimate offspring is a power of distinguishing right from wrong, which power applied to works of art is denominated taste. Let me then, without further introduction, enter upon an examination whether taste be so far beyond our reach as to be unattainable by care, or be so very vague and capricious that no care ought to be employed about it.

It has been the fate of arts to be enveloped in mysterious and incomprehensible language, as if it was thought necessary that even the terms should correspond to the idea entertained of the instability and uncertainty of the rules which they expressed.

To speak of genius and taste as any way connected with reason or common sense, would be, in the opinion of some towering talkers, to speak like a man who possessed neither, who had never felt that enthusiasm, or, to use their own inflated language, was never warmed by that Promethean fire, which animates the canvas and vivifies the marble.

If, in order to be intelligible, I appear to degrade art by bringing her down from her visionary situation in the clouds, it is only to give her a more solid mansion upon the earth. It is necessary that at some time or other we should see things as they really are, and not impose on ourselves by that false magnitude with which objects appear when viewed indistinctly as through a mist.

We will allow a poet to express his meaning, when his meaning is not well known to himself, with a certain degree of obscurity, as it is one source of the sublime. But when, in plain prose, we gravely talk of courting the muse in shady bowers, waiting the call and inspiration of genius, finding out where he inhabits, and where he is to be invoked with the greatest success; of attending to times and seasons when the imagination shoots with the greatest vigour, whether at the summer solstice or the equinox, sagaciously observing how much the wild freedom and liberty of imagination is cramped by attention to established rules, and how this same imagination begins to grow dim in advanced age, smothered and deadened by too much judgment. When we talk such language, or entertain such sentiments as these, we generally rest contented with mere words, or at best entertain notions not only groundless, but pernicious.

If all this means what it is very possible was originally intended only to be meant, that in order to cultivate an art, a man secludes himself from the commerce of the world, and retires into the country at particular seasons; or that at one time of the year his body is in better health, and consequently his mind fitter for the business of hard thinking than at another time; or that the mind may be fatigued and grow confused by long and unremitted application; this I can understand. I can likewise believe that a man eminent when young for possessing poetical imagination, may, from having taken another road, so neglect its cultivation as to show less of its powers in his latter life. But I am persuaded that scarce a poet is to be found, from Homer down to Dryden, who preserved a sound mind in a sound body, and continued practising his profession to the very last, whose later works are not as replete with the fire of imagination as those which were produced in his more youthful days.

To understand literally these metaphors or ideas expressed in poetical language, seems to be equally absurd as to conclude that because painters sometimes represent poets writing from the dictates of a little winged boy or genius, that this same genius did really inform him in a whisper what he was to write, and that he is himself but a mere machine, unconscious of the operations of his own mind.

Opinions generally received and floating in the world, whether true or false, we naturally adopt and make our own; they may be considered as a kind of inheritance to which we succeed and are tenants for life, and which we leave to our posterity very near in the condition in which we received it; not much being in any one man's power either to impair or improve it.

The greatest part of these opinions, like current coin in its circulation, we are obliged to take without weighing or examining; but by this inevitable inattention, many adulterated pieces are received, which, when we seriously estimate our wealth, we must throw away. So the collector of popular opinions, when he embodies his knowledge, and forms a system, must separate those which are true from those which are only plausible. But it becomes more peculiarly a duty to the professors of art not to let any opinions relating to that art pass unexamined. The caution and circumspection required in such examination we shall presently have an opportunity of explaining.

Genius and taste, in their common acceptation, appear to be very nearly related; the difference lies only in this, that genius has superadded to it a habit or power of execution. Or we may say, that taste, when this power is added, changes its name, and is called genius. They both, in the popular opinion, pretend to an entire exemption from the restraint of rules. It is supposed that their powers are intuitive; that under the name of genius great works are produced, and under the name of taste an exact judgment is given, without our knowing why, and without being under the least obligation to reason, precept, or experience.

One can scarce state these opinions without exposing their absurdity, yet they are constantly in the mouths of men, and particularly of artists. They who have thought seriously on this subject, do not carry the point so far; yet I am persuaded, that even among those few who may be called thinkers, the prevalent opinion gives less than it ought to the powers of reason; and considers the principles of taste, which give all their authority to the rules of art, as more fluctuating, and as having less solid foundations than we shall find, upon examination, they really have.

The common saying, that tastes are not to be disputed, owes its influence, and its general reception, to the same error which leads us to imagine it of too high original to submit to the authority of an earthly tribunal. It will likewise correspond with the notions of those who consider it as a mere phantom of the imagination, so devoid of substance as to elude all criticism.

We often appear to differ in sentiments from each other, merely from the inaccuracy of terms, as we are not obliged to speak always with critical exactness. Something of this too may arise from want of words in the language to express the more nice discriminations which a deep investigation discovers. A great deal, however, of this difference vanishes when each opinion is tolerably explained and understood by constancy and precision in the use of terms.

We apply the term taste to that act of the mind by which we like or dislike, whatever be the subject. Our judgment upon an airy nothing, a fancy which has no foundation, is called by the same name which we give to our determination concerning those truths which refer to the most general and most unalterable principles of human nature, to works which are only to be produced by the greatest efforts of the human understanding. However inconvenient this may be, we are obliged to take words as we find them; all we can do is to distinguish the things to which they are applied.

We may let pass those things which are at once subjects of taste and sense, and which having as much certainty as the senses themselves, give no occasion to inquiry or dispute. The natural appetite or taste of the human mind is for truth; whether that truth results from the real agreement or equality of original ideas among themselves; from the agreement of the representation of any object with the thing represented; or from the correspondence of the several parts of any arrangement with each other. It is the very same taste which relishes a demonstration in geometry, that is pleased with the resemblance of a picture to an original, and touched with the harmony of music.

All these have unalterable and fixed foundations in nature, and are therefore equally investigated by reason, and known by study; some with more, some with less clearness, but all exactly in the same way. A picture that is unlike, is false. Disproportionate ordinance of parts is not right because it cannot be true until it ceases to be a contradiction to assert that the parts have no relation to the whole. Colouring is true where it is naturally adapted to the eye, from brightness, from softness, from harmony, from resemblance; because these agree with their object, nature, and therefore are true: as true as mathematical demonstration; but known to be true only to those who study these things.

But besides real, there is also apparent truth, or opinion, or prejudice. With regard to real truth, when it is known, the taste which conforms to it is, and must be, uniform. With regard to the second sort of truth, which may be called truth upon sufferance, or truth by courtesy, it is not fixed, but variable. However, whilst these opinions and prejudices on which it is founded continue, they operate as truth; and the art, whose office it is to please the mind, as well as instruct it, must direct itself according to opinion, or it will not attain its end.

In proportion as these prejudices are known to be generally diffused, or long received, the taste which conforms to them approaches nearer to certainty, and to a sort of resemblance to real science, even where opinions are found to be no better than prejudices. And since they deserve, on account of their duration and extent, to be considered as really true, they become capable of no small decree of stability and determination by their permanent and uniform nature.

As these prejudices become more narrow, more local, more transitory, this secondary taste becomes more and more fantastical; recedes from real science; is less to be approved by reason, and less followed in practice; though in no case perhaps to be wholly neglected, where it does not stand, as it sometimes does, in direct defiance of the most respectable opinions received amongst mankind.

Having laid down these positions, I shall proceed with less method, because less will serve, to explain and apply them.

We will take it for granted that reason is something invariable and fixed in the nature of things; and without endeavouring to go back to an account of first principles, which for ever will elude our search, we will conclude that whatever goes under the name of taste, which we can fairly bring under the dominion of reason, must be considered as equally exempt from change. If therefore, in the course of this inquiry, we can show that there are rules for the conduct of the artist which are fixed and invariable, it implies, of course, that the art of the connoisseur, or, in other words, taste, has likewise invariable principles.

Of the judgment which we make on the works of art, and the preference that we give to one class of art over another, if a reason be demanded, the question is perhaps evaded by answering, "I judge from my taste"; but it does not follow that a better answer cannot be given, though for common gazers this may be sufficient. Every man is not obliged to investigate the causes of his approbation or dislike.

The arts would lie open for ever to caprice and casualty, if those who are to judge of their excellences had no settled principles by which they are to regulate their decisions, and the merit or defect of performances were to be determined by unguided fancy. And indeed we may venture to assert that whatever speculative knowledge is necessary to the artist, is equally and indispensably necessary to the connoisseur.

The first idea that occurs in the consideration of what is fixed in art, or in taste, is that presiding principle of which I have so frequently spoken in former discourses, the general idea of nature. The beginning, the middle, and the end of everything that is valuable in taste, is comprised in the knowledge of what is truly nature; for whatever ideas are not conformable to those of nature, or universal opinion, must be considered as more or less capricious.

The idea of nature comprehending not only the forms which nature produces, but also the nature and internal fabric and organisation, as I may call it, of the human mind and imagination: general ideas, beauty, or nature, are but different ways of expressing the same thing, whether we apply these terms to statues, poetry, or picture. Deformity is not nature, but an accidental deviation from her accustomed practice. This general idea therefore ought to be called nature, and nothing else, correctly speaking, has a right to that name. But we are so far from speaking, in common conversation, with any such accuracy, that, on the contrary, when we criticise Rembrandt and other Dutch painters, who introduced into their historical pictures exact representations of individual objects with all their imperfections, we say, though it is not in a good taste, yet it is nature.

This misapplication of terms must be very often perplexing to the young student. Is not, he may say, art an imitation of nature? Must he not, therefore, who imitates her with the greatest fidelity be the best artist? By this mode of reasoning Rembrandt has a higher place than Raffaelle. But a very little reflection will serve to show us that these particularities cannot be nature: for how can that be the nature of man, in which no two individuals are the same?

It plainly appears that as a work is conducted under the influence of general ideas or partial it is principally to be considered as the effect of a good or a bad taste.

As beauty therefore does not consist in taking what lies immediately before you, so neither, in our pursuit of taste, are those opinions which we first received and adopted the best choice, or the most natural to the mind and imagination.

In the infancy of our knowledge we seize with greediness the good that is within our reach; it is by after-consideration, and in consequence of discipline, that we refuse the present for a greater good at a distance. The nobility or elevation of all arts, like the excellence of virtue itself, consists in adopting this enlarged and comprehensive idea, and all criticism built upon the more confined view of what is natural, may properly be called shallow criticism, rather than false; its defect is that the truth is not sufficiently extensive.

It has sometimes happened that some of the greatest men in our art have been betrayed into errors by this confined mode of reasoning. Poussin, who, upon the whole, may be produced as an instance of attention to the most enlarged and extensive ideas of nature, from not having settled principles on this point, has in one instance at least, I think, deserted truth for prejudice. He is said to have vindicated the conduct of Julio Romano, for his inattention to the masses of light and shade, or grouping the figures, in the battle of Constantine, as if designedly neglected, the better to correspond with the hurry and confusion of a battle. Poussin's own conduct in his representations of Bacchanalian triumphs and sacrifices, makes us more easily give credit to this report, since in such subjects, as well indeed as in many others, it was too much his own practice. The best apology we can make for this conduct is what proceeds from the association of our ideas, the prejudice we have in favour of antiquity. Poussin's works, as I have formerly observed, have very much the air of the ancient manner of painting, in which there are not the least traces to make us think that what we call the keeping, the composition of light and shade, or distribution of the work into masses, claimed any part of their attention. But surely whatever apology we may find out for this neglect, it ought to be ranked among the defects of Poussin, as well as of the antique paintings; and the moderns have a right to that praise which is their due, for having given so pleasing an addition to the splendour of the art.

Perhaps no apology ought to be received for offences committed against the vehicle (whether it be the organ of seeing or of hearing) by which our pleasures are conveyed to the mind. We must take the same care that the eye be not perplexed and distracted by a confusion of equal parts, or equal lights, as of offending it by an unharmonious mixture of colours. We may venture to be more confident of the truth of this observation, since we find that Shakespeare, on a parallel occasion, has made Hamlet recommend to the players a precept of the same kind, never to offend the ear by harsh sounds:—"In the very torrent, tempest, and whirlwind of your passions," says he, "you must beget a temperance that may give it smoothness." And yet, at the same time, he very justly observes, "The end of playing, both at the first and now, is to hold, as it were, the mirror up to nature." No one can deny but that violent passions will naturally emit harsh and disagreeable tones; yet this great poet and critic thought that this imitation of nature would cost too much, if purchased at the expense of disagreeable sensations, or, as he expresses it, of "splitting the ear." The poet and actor, as well as the painter of genius who is well acquainted with all the variety and sources of pleasure in the mind and imagination, has little regard or attention to common nature, or creeping after common sense. By overleaping those narrow bounds, he more effectually seizes the whole mind, and more powerfully accomplishes his purpose. This success is ignorantly imagined to proceed from inattention to all rules, and in defiance of reason and judgment; whereas it is in truth acting according to the best rules, and the justest reason.

He who thinks nature, in the narrow sense of the word, is alone to be followed, will produce but a scanty entertainment for the imagination: everything is to be done with which it is natural for the mind to be pleased, whether it proceeds from simplicity or variety, uniformity or irregularity: whether the scenes are familiar or exotic; rude and wild, or enriched and cultivated; for it is natural for the mind to be pleased with all these in their turn. In short, whatever pleases has in it what is analogous to the mind, and is therefore, in the highest and best sense of the word, natural.

It is this sense of nature or truth which ought more particularly to be cultivated by the professors of art; and it may be observed that many wise and learned men, who have accustomed their minds to admit nothing for truth but what can be proved by mathematical demonstration, have seldom any relish for those arts which address themselves to the fancy, the rectitude and truth of which is known by another kind of proof: and we may add that the acquisition of this knowledge requires as much circumspection and sagacity, as to attain those truths which are more open to demonstration. Reason must ultimately determine our choice on every occasion; but this reason may still be exerted ineffectually by applying to taste principles which, though right as far as they go, yet do not reach the object. No man, for instance, can deny that it seems at first view very reasonable, that a statue which is to carry down to posterity the resemblance of an individual should be dressed in the fashion of the times, in the dress which he himself wore: this would certainly be true if the dress were part of the man. But after a time the dress is only an amusement for an antiquarian; and if it obstructs the general design of the piece, it is to be disregarded by the artist. Common sense must here give way to a higher sense.

In the naked form, and in the disposition of the drapery, the difference between one artist and another is principally seen. But if he is compelled to the modern dress, the naked form is entirely hid, and the drapery is already disposed by the skill of the tailor. Were a Phidias to obey such absurd commands, he would please no more than an ordinary sculptor; since, in the inferior parts of every art, the learned and the ignorant are nearly upon a level.

These were probably among the reasons that induced the sculptor of that wonderful figure of Laocoon to exhibit him naked, notwithstanding he was surprised in the act of sacrificing to Apollo, and consequently ought to be shown in his sacerdotal habits, if those greater reasons had not preponderated. Art is not yet in so high estimation with us as to obtain so great a sacrifice as the ancients made, especially the Grecians, who suffered themselves to be represented naked, whether they were generals, lawgivers, or kings.

Under this head of balancing and choosing the greater reason, or of two evils taking the least, we may consider the conduct of Rubens in the Luxembourg gallery, of mixing allegorical figures with representations of real personages, which, though acknowledged to be a fault, yet, if the artist considered himself as engaged to furnish this gallery with a rich and splendid ornament, this could not be done, at least in an equal degree, without peopling the air and water with these allegorical figures: he therefore accomplished that he purposes. In this case all lesser considerations, which tend to obstruct the great end of the work, must yield and give way.

If it is objected that Rubens judged ill at first in thinking it necessary to make his work so very ornamental, this brings the question upon new ground. It was his peculiar style; he could paint in no other; and he was selected for that work, probably, because it was his style. Nobody will dispute but some of the best of the Roman or Bolognian schools would have produced a more learned and more noble work.

This leads us to another important province of taste, of weighing the value of the different classes of the art, and of estimating them accordingly.

All arts have means within them of applying themselves with success both to the intellectual and sensitive part of our natures. It can be no dispute, supposing both these means put in practice with equal abilities, to which we ought to give the preference: to him who represents the heroic arts and more dignified passions of man, or to him who, by the help of meretricious ornaments, however elegant and graceful, captivates the sensuality, as it may be called, of our taste. Thus the Roman and Bolognian schools are reasonably preferred to the Venetian, Flemish, or Dutch schools, as they address themselves to our best and noblest faculties.

Well-turned periods in eloquence, or harmony of numbers in poetry, which are in those arts what colouring is in painting, however highly we may esteem them, can never be considered as of equal importance with the art of unfolding truths that are useful to mankind, and which make us better or wiser. Nor can those works which remind us of the poverty and meanness of our nature, be considered as of equal rank with what excites ideas of grandeur, or raises and dignifies humanity; or, in the words of a late poet, which makes the beholder learn to venerate himself as man.

It is reason and good sense therefore which ranks and estimates every art, and every part of that art, according to its importance, from the painter of animated down to inanimated nature. We will not allow a man, who shall prefer the inferior style, to say it is his taste; taste here has nothing, or at least ought to have nothing to do with the question. He wants not taste, but sense, and soundness of judgment.

Indeed, perfection in an inferior style may be reasonably preferred to mediocrity in the highest walks of art. A landscape of Claude Lorraine may be preferred to a history of Luca Jordano; but hence appears the necessity of the connoisseur's knowing in what consists the excellence of each class, in order to judge how near it approaches to perfection.

Even in works of the same kind, as in history painting, which is composed of various parts, excellence of an inferior species, carried to a very high degree, will make a work very valuable, and in some measure compensate for the absence of the higher kind of merits. It is the duty of the connoisseur to know and esteem, as much as it may deserve, every part of painting; he will not then think even Bassano unworthy of his notice, who, though totally devoid of expression, sense, grace, or elegance, may be esteemed on account of his admirable taste of colours, which, in his best works, are little inferior to those of Titian.

Since I have mentioned Bassano, we must do him likewise the justice to acknowledge that, though he did not aspire to the dignity of expressing the characters and passions of men, yet, with respect to the facility and truth in his manner of touching animals of all kinds, and giving them what painters call their character, few have ever excelled him.

To Bassano we may add Paul Veronese and Tintoret, for their entire inattention to what is justly esteemed the most essential part of our art, the expression of the passions. Notwithstanding these glaring deficiencies, we justly esteem their works; but it must be remembered that they do not please from those defects, but from their great excellences of another kind, and in spite of such transgressions. These excellences, too, as far as they go, are founded in the truth of general nature. They tell the truth, though not the whole truth.

By these considerations, which can never be too frequently impressed, may be obviated two errors which I observed to have been, formerly at least, the most prevalent, and to be most injurious to artists: that of thinking taste and genius to have nothing to do with reason, and that of taking particular living objects for nature.

I shall now say something on that part of taste which, as I have hinted to you before, does not belong so much to the external form of things, but is addressed to the mind, and depends on its original frame, or, to use the expression, the organisation of the soul; I mean the imagination and the passions. The principles of these are as invariable as the former, and are to be known and reasoned upon in the same manner, by an appeal to common sense deciding upon the common feelings of mankind. This sense, and these feelings, appear to me of equal authority, and equally conclusive.

Now this appeal implies a general uniformity and agreement in the minds of men. It would be else an idle and vain endeavour to establish rules of art; it would be pursuing a phantom to attempt to move affections with which we were entirely unacquainted. We have no reason to suspect there is a greater difference between our minds than between our forms, of which, though there are no two alike, yet there is a general similitude that goes through the whole race of mankind; and those who have cultivated their taste can distinguish what is beautiful or deformed, or, in other words, what agrees with or what deviates from the general idea of nature, in one case as well as in the other.

The internal fabric of our mind, as well as the external form of our bodies, being nearly uniform, it seems then to follow, of course, that as the imagination is incapable of producing anything originally of itself, and can only vary and combine these ideas with which it is furnished by means of the senses, there will be, of course, an agreement in the imaginations as in the senses of men. There being this agreement, it follows that in all cases, in our lightest amusements as well as in our most serious actions and engagements of life, we must regulate our affections of every kind by that of others. The well-disciplined mind acknowledges this authority, and submits its own opinion to the public voice.

It is from knowing what are the general feelings and passions of mankind that we acquire a true idea of what imagination is; though it appears as if we had nothing to do but to consult our own particular sensations, and these were sufficient to ensure us from all error and mistake.

A knowledge of the disposition and character of the human mind can be acquired only by experience: a great deal will be learned, I admit, by a habit of examining what passes in our bosoms, what are our own motives of action, and of what kind of sentiments we are conscious on any occasion. We may suppose a uniformity, and conclude that the same effect will be produced by the same cause in the minds of others. This examination will contribute to suggest to us matters of inquiry; but we can never be sure that our own sensations are true and right till they are confirmed by more extensive observation.

One man opposing another determines nothing but a general union of minds, like a general combination of the forces of all mankind, makes a strength that is irresistible. In fact, as he who does not know himself does not know others, so it may be said with equal truth, that he who does not know others knows himself but very imperfectly.

A man who thinks he is guarding himself against Prejudices by resisting the authority of others, leaves open every avenue to singularity, vanity, self-conceit, obstinacy, and many other vices, all tending to warp the judgment and prevent the natural operation of his faculties.

This submission to others is a deference which we owe, and indeed are forced involuntarily to pay.

In fact we are never satisfied with our opinions till they are ratified and confirmed by the suffrages of the rest of mankind. We dispute and wrangle for ever; we endeavour to get men to come to us when we do not go to them.

He therefore who is acquainted with the works which have pleased different ages and different countries, and has formed his opinion on them, has more materials and more means of knowing what is analogous to the mind of man than he who is conversant only with the works of his own age or country. What has pleased, and continues to please, is likely to please again: hence are derived the rules of art, and on this immovable foundation they must ever stand.

This search and study of the history of the mind ought not to be confined to one art only. It is by the analogy that one art bears to another that many things are ascertained which either were but faintly seen, or, perhaps, would not have been discovered at all if the inventor had not received the first hints from the practices of a sister art on a similar occasion. The frequent allusions which every man who treats of any art is obliged to draw from others in order to illustrate and confirm his principles, sufficiently show their near connection and inseparable relation.

All arts having the same general end, which is to please, and addressing themselves to the same faculties through the medium of the senses, it follows that their rules and principles must have as great affinity as the different materials and the different organs or vehicles by which they pass to the mind will permit them to retain.

We may therefore conclude that the real substance, as it may be called, of what goes under the name of taste, is fixed and established in the nature of things; that there are certain and regular causes by which the imagination and passions of men are affected; and that the knowledge of these causes is acquired by a laborious and diligent investigation of nature, and by the same slow progress as wisdom or knowledge of every kind, however instantaneous its operations may appear when thus acquired.

It has been often observed that the good and virtuous man alone can acquire this true or just relish, even of works of art. This opinion will not appear entirely without foundation when we consider that the same habit of mind which is acquired by our search after truth in the more serious duties of life, is only transferred to the pursuit of lighter amusements: the same disposition, the same desire to find something steady, substantial, and durable, on which the mind can lean, as it were, and rest with safety. The subject only is changed. We pursue the same method in our search after the idea of beauty and perfection in each; of virtue, by looking forwards beyond ourselves to society, and to the whole; of arts, by extending our views in the same manner to all ages and all times.

Every art, like our own, has in its composition fluctuating as well as fixed principles. It is an attentive inquiry into their difference that will enable us to determine how far we are influenced by custom and habit, and what is fixed in the nature of things.

To distinguish how much has solid foundation, we may have recourse to the same proof by which some hold wit ought to be tried— whether it preserves itself when translated. That wit is false which can subsist only in one language; and that picture which pleases only one age or one nation, owes its reception to some local or accidental association of ideas.

We may apply this to every custom and habit of life. Thus the general principles of urbanity, politeness, or civility, have been ever the same in all nations; but the mode in which they are dressed is continually varying. The general idea of showing respect is by making yourself less: but the manner, whether by bowing the body, kneeling, prostration, pulling off the upper part of our dress, or taking away the lower, is a matter of habit. It would be unjust to conclude that all ornaments, because they were at first arbitrarily contrived, are therefore undeserving of our attention; on the contrary, he who neglects the cultivation of those ornaments, acts contrarily to nature and reason. As life would be imperfect without its highest ornaments, the arts, so these arts themselves would be imperfect without *their* ornaments.

Though we by no means ought to rank these with positive and substantial beauties, yet it must be allowed that a knowledge of both is essentially requisite towards forming a complete, whole, and perfect taste. It is in reality from the ornaments that arts receive their peculiar character and complexion; we may add that in them we find the characteristical mark of a national taste, as by throwing up a feather in the air we know which way the wind blows, better than by a more heavy matter.

The striking distinction between the works of the Roman, Bolognian, and Venetian schools, consists more in that general effect which is produced by colours than in the more profound excellences of the art; at least it is from thence that each is distinguished and known at first sight. As it is the ornaments rather than the proportions of architecture which at the first glance distinguish the different orders from each other; the Doric is known by its triglyphs, the Ionic by its volutes, and the Corinthian by its acanthus.

What distinguishes oratory from a cold narration, is a more liberal though chaste use of these ornaments which go under the name of figurative and metaphorical expressions; and poetry distinguishes itself from oratory by words and expressions still more ardent and glowing. What separates and distinguishes poetry is more particularly the ornament of *verse*; it is this which gives it its character, and is an essential, without which it cannot exist. Custom has appropriated different metre to different kinds of composition, in which the world is not perfectly agreed. In England the dispute is not yet settled which is to be preferred, rhyme or blank verse. But however we disagree about what these metrical ornaments shall be, that some metre is essentially necessary is universally acknowledged.

In poetry or eloquence, to determine how far figurative or meta-phorical language may proceed, and when it begins to be affectation or beside the truth, must be determined by taste, though this taste we must never forget is regulated and formed by the presiding feelings of mankind, by those works which have approved themselves to all times and all persons.

Thus, though eloquence has undoubtedly an essential and intrin-sic excellence, and immovable principles common to all languages, founded in the nature of our passions and affections, yet it has its ornaments and modes of address which are merely arbitrary. What is approved in the Eastern nations as grand and majestic, would be con-sidered by the Greeks and Romans as turgid and inflated; and they, in return, would be thought by the Orientals to express themselves in a cold and insipid manner.

We may add likewise to the credit of ornaments, that it is by their means that art itself accomplishes its purpose. Fresnoy calls colour-ing, which is one of the chief ornaments of painting, *lena sororis*, that which procures lovers and admirers to the more valuable excellences of the art.

It appears to be the same right turn of mind which enables a man to acquire the *truth*, or the just idea of what is right in the ornaments, as in the more stable principles of art. It has still the same centre of perfection, though it is the centre of a smaller circle.

To illustrate this by the fashion of dress, in which there is allowed to be a good or, bad taste. The component parts of dress are continually changing from great to little, from short to long, but the general form still remains; it is still the same general dress which is comparatively fixed, though on a very slender foundation, but it is on this which fashion must rest. He who invents with the most success, or dresses in, the best taste, would probably, from the same sagacity employed to greater purposes, have discovered equal skill, or have formed the same correct taste in the highest labours of art.

I have mentioned taste in dress, which is certainly one of the lowest subjects to which this word is applied; yet, as I have before observed, there is a right even here, however narrow its foundation respecting the fashion of any particular nation. But we have still more slender means of determining, in regard to the different customs of different ages or countries, to which to give the preference, since they seem to be all equally removed from nature.

If an European, when he has cut off his beard, and put false hair on his head, or bound up his own natural hair in regular hard knots, as unlike nature as he can possibly make it; and having rendered them immovable by the help of the fat of hogs, has covered the whole with flour, laid on by a machine with the utmost regularity; if, when thus attired he issues forth, he meets a Cherokee Indian, who has bestowed as much time at his toilet, and laid on with equal care and attention his yellow and red ochre on particular parts of his forehead or cheeks, as he judges most becoming; whoever despises the other for this attention to the fashion of his country, whichever of these two first feels himself provoked to laugh, is the barbarian.

All these fashions are very innocent, neither worth disquisition, nor any endeavour to alter them, as the change would, in all probability, be equally distant from nature. The only circumstances against which indignation may reasonably be moved, are where the operation is painful or destructive of health, such as is practised at Otahaiti, and the straight lacing of the English ladies; of the last of which, how destructive it must be to health and long life, the professor of anatomy took an opportunity of proving a few days since in this Academy.

It is in dress as in things of greater consequence. Fashions originate from those only who have the high and powerful advantages of rank, birth, and fortune; as many of the ornaments of art, those at least for which no reason can be given, are transmitted to us, are adopted, and acquire their consequence from the company in which we have been used to see them. As Greece and Rome are the fountains from whence have flowed all kinds of excellence, to that veneration which they have a right to claim for the pleasure and knowledge which they have afforded us, we voluntarily add our approbation of every ornament and every custom that belonged to them, even to the fashion of their dress. For it may be observed that, not satisfied with them in their own place, we make no difficulty of dressing statues of modern heroes or senators in the fashion of the Roman armour or peaceful robe; we go so far as hardly to bear a statue in any other drapery.

The figures of the great men of those nations have come down to us in sculpture. In sculpture remain almost all the excellent specimens of ancient art. We have so far associated personal dignity to the persons thus represented, and the truth of art to their manner of representation, that it is not in our power any longer to separate them. This is not so in painting; because, having no excellent ancient portraits, that connection was never formed. Indeed, we could no more venture to paint a general officer in a Roman military habit, than we could make a statue in the present uniform. But since we have no ancient portraits, to show how ready we are to adopt those kind of prejudices, we make the best authority among the moderns serve the same purpose. The great variety of excellent portraits with which Vandyke has enriched this nation, we are not content to admire for their real excellence, but extend our approbation even to the dress which happened to be the fashion of that age. We all very well remember how common it was a few years ago for portraits to be drawn in this Gothic dress, and this custom is not yet entirely laid aside. By this means it must be acknowledged very ordinary pictures acquired something of the air and effect of the works of Vandyke, and appeared therefore at first sight to be better pictures than they really were; they appeared so, however, to those only who had the means of making this association, for when made, it was irresistible. But this association is nature, and refers to that Secondary truth that comes from conformity to general prejudice and opinion; it is therefore not merely fantastical. Besides the prejudice which we have in favour of ancient dresses, there may be likewise other reasons, amongst which we may justly rank the simplicity of them, consisting of little more than one single piece of drapery, without those whimsical capricious forms by which all other dresses are embarrassed.

Thus, though it is from the prejudice we have in favour of the ancients, who have taught us architecture, that we have adopted likewise their ornaments; and though we are satisfied that neither nature nor reason is the foundation of those beauties which we imagine we see in that art, yet if any one persuaded of this truth should, therefore, invent new orders of equal beauty, which we will suppose to be possible, yet they would not please, nor ought he to complain, since the old has that great advantage of having custom and prejudice on its side. In this case we leave what has every prejudice in its favour to take that which will have no advantage over what we have left, but novelty, which soon destroys itself, and, at any rate, is but a weak antagonist against custom.

These ornaments, having the right of possession, ought not to be removed but to make room for not only what has higher pretensions, but such pretensions as will balance the evil and confusion which innovation always brings with it.

To this we may add, even the durability of the materials will often contribute to give a superiority to one object over another. Ornaments in buildings, with which taste is principally concerned, are composed of materials which last longer than those of which dress is composed; it, therefore, makes higher pretensions to our favour and prejudice.

Some attention is surely required to what we can no more get rid of than we can go out of ourselves. We are creatures of prejudice; we neither can nor ought to eradicate it; we must only regulate, it by reason, which regulation by reason is, indeed, little more than obliging the lesser, the focal and temporary prejudices, to give way to those which are more durable and lasting.

He, therefore, who in his practice of portrait painting wishes to dignify his subject, which we will suppose to be a lady, will not paint her in the modern dress, the familiarity of which alone is sufficient to destroy all dignity. He takes care that his work shall correspond to those ideas and that imagination which he knows will regulate the judgment of others, and, therefore, dresses his figure something with the general air of the antique for the sake of dignity, and preserves something of the modern for the sake of likeness. By this conduct his works correspond with those prejudices which we have in favour of what we continually see; and the relish of the antique simplicity corresponds with what we may call the, more learned and scientific prejudice.

There was a statue made not long since of Voltaire, which the sculptor, not having that respect for the prejudices of mankind which he ought to have, has made entirely naked, and as meagre and emaciated as the original is said to be. The consequence is what might be expected; it has remained in the sculptor's shop, though it was intended as a public ornament and a public honour to Voltaire, as it was procured at the expense of his contemporary wits and admirers.

Whoever would reform a nation, supposing a bad taste to prevail in it, will not accomplish his purpose by going directly against the stream of their prejudices. Men's minds must be prepared to receive what is new to them. Reformation is a work of time. A national taste, however wrong it may be, cannot be totally change at once; we must yield a little to the prepossession which has taken hold on the mind, and we may then bring people to adopt what would offend them if endeavoured to be introduced by storm. When Battisto Franco was employed, in conjunction with Titian, Paul Veronese, and Tintoret, to adorn the library of St. Mark, his work, Vasari says, gave less satisfaction than any of the others: the dry manner of the Roman school was very ill calculated to please eyes that had been accustomed to the luxuriance, splendour, and richness of Venetian colouring. Had the Romans been the judges of this work, probably the determination would have been just contrary; for in the more noble parts of the art Battisto Franco was, perhaps, not inferior to any of his rivals.

* * * * *

Gentlemen,—It has been the main scope and principal end of this discourse to demonstrate the reality of a standard in taste, as well as in corporeal beauty; that a false or depraved taste is a thing as well known, as easily discovered, as anything that is deformed, misshapen, or wrong in our form or outward make; and that this knowledge is derived from the uniformity of sentiments among mankind, from whence proceeds the knowledge of what are the general habits of nature, the result of which is an idea of perfect beauty.

If what has been advanced be true, that besides this beauty or truth which is formed on the uniform eternal and immutable laws of nature, and which of necessity can be but one; that besides this one immutable verity there are likewise what we have called apparent or secondary truths proceeding from local and temporary prejudices, fancies, fashions, or accidental connection of ideas; if it appears that these last have still their foundation, however slender, in the original fabric of our minds, it follows that all these truths or beauties deserve and require the attention of the artist in proportion to their stability or duration, or as their influence is more or less extensive. And let me add that as they ought not to pass their just bounds, so neither do they, in a well-regulated taste, at all prevent or weaken the influence of these general principles, which alone can give to art its true and permanent dignity.

To form this just taste is undoubtedly in your own power, but it is to reason and philosophy that you must have recourse; from them we must borrow the balance by which is to be weighed and estimated the value of every pretension that intrudes itself on your notice.

The general objection which is made to the introduction of philosophy into the regions of taste is, that it checks and restrains the flights of the imagination, and gives that timidity which an over-carefulness not to err or act contrary to reason is likely to produce.

It is not so. Fear is neither reason nor philosophy. The true spirit of philosophy by giving knowledge gives a manly confidence, and substitutes rational firmness in the place of vain presumption. A man of real taste is always a man of judgment in other respects; and those inventions which either disdain or shrink from reason, are generally, I fear, more like the dreams of a distempered brain than the exalted enthusiasm of a sound and true genius. In the midst of the highest flights of fancy or imagination, reason ought to preside from first to last, though I admit her more powerful operation is upon reflection.

I cannot help adding that some of the greatest names of antiquity, and those who have most distinguished themselves in works of genius and imagination, were equally eminent for their critical skill. Plato, Aristotle, Cicero, and Horace; and among the moderns, Boileau, Corneille, Pope, and Dryden, are at least instances of genius not being destroyed by attention or subjection to rules and science. I should hope, therefore, that the natural consequence likewise of what has been said would be to excite in you a desire of knowing the principles and conduct of the great masters of our art, and respect and veneration for them when known.